ALMODÓVAR
A RETROSPECTIVE

“LUCKILY, NATURE HAS ENDOWED ME WITH AN IRRATIONAL CURIOSITY FOR EVEN THE MOST TRIVIAL THINGS. THAT SAVES ME. CURIOSITY IS THE ONLY THING THAT KEEPS ME AFLOAT. OH, AND VOCATION.”

ALMODÓVAR
A RETROSPECTIVE

Pau Gómez

FOREWORD BY ANTONIO BANDERAS
AFTERWORD BY CECILIA ROTH

G:

First published in the USA in 2024 by
Gemini Adult Books Ltd,
part of the Gemini Books Group
Based in Woodbridge and London
Marine House, Tide Mill Way, Woodbridge
Suffolk, IP12 1AP
www.geminibooks.com

Cover designed by Steve O Connell

Front cover photograph kindly supplied by Outumuro Estudio © Manuel Outumuro

Hardback ISBN 9781786751393

Bound and printed in China

10 9 8 7 6 5 4 3 2 1

Designed by Adelle Mahoney

CONTENTS

FOREWORD

In 2002, twelve years after our last collaboration on *Tie Me Up! Tie Me Down!*, Pedro and I had our first conversation about *The Skin I Live In* at the Cannes Film Festival. He told me that he had read Thierry Jonquet's novel and that he was going to start the process of adapting it to film, and that he was interested in me playing Doctor Ledgard. In all that time without working together, he had called me a couple of times, but I always had a contract that committed me for a long time to another film and it was impossible for me to dedicate myself to Pedro's project. Finally, one day in early 2010, he called me on the phone as I was leaving a rehearsal on Broadway, and he said, 'The time has come.'

I've always thought that the only time an actor is also a spectator is when he reads a script for the first time. *The Skin I Live In* had a huge impact on me, and I immediately felt that it was a project tailor-made for Almodóvar, because only he could tell that story and tell it the way that the script reflected, with such freedom, using the premise of the novel as an inspiration and a starting point from which to create something totally different and genuine. I was very clear that I had to approach my character from a gestural economy, that he should do everything he does with absolute naturalness and turn him into a blank screen where the audience could express their concerns. I soon realised that this was the right project for our reunion, and I knew that the long wait had been worth it.

I've had the good fortune to work with Pedro Almodóvar many times, with wonderful characters who somehow always had some particularity that made them strangely fascinating (in *Matador* my character, Ángel, suffered from a kind of vertigo that gave him visions of the future!). His system of work is long and complex, but it always manages to bring out the best in you, and that is something for which I am deeply grateful.

However, even if it had never been like that and our paths had never crossed, I would have to thank him for all the good he has done for cinema – in particular, for Spanish cinema, although sometimes it is hard to recognise it – and the enormous and well-deserved admiration he has all over the world. Fortunately for me, when we met in 1982 to shoot *Labyrinth of Passion*, Pedro told me that my real name – José Antonio Domínguez – sounded like a bullfighter to him, and that, if I agreed, he preferred to use my middle name and surname – Bandera – in the plural, because he liked it very much. 'They're the credits of your film, so go ahead,' I told him.

The rest... is history.

Antonio Banderas

INTRODUCTION

The Long and Painful Road to Glory

Few contemporary filmmakers have exposed and given so much of their emotional life to their art as Pedro Almodóvar. From his first film, *Pepi, Luci, Bom and Other Girls Like Mom* (1980) to the most recent, *Parallel Mothers* (2021), his cinema has evolved through various stages without ever losing sight of a series of common and universally constant themes, arising from a mixture of his own experiences, his cultural influences, and his very particular way of seeing and understanding the world. It is undeniable that the early wild and experimental works have given way to others that are more serene and introspective, a reasonable transition for an auteur whose filmmaking changes and adapts to the different tides in a life. But the amazing thing about Almodóvar is his ability to imbue films four decades apart with the same spirit. A spirit that continues to be inimitable, and thanks to which he has become one of the most important filmmakers of the last four decades.

Pedro Almodóvar's works have achieved worldwide recognition, based on universal stories with a strong influence of Spanish popular culture. The identity of his characters, the constant references to the rural environment and the recurrent use of iconographies and the traditions of his country – such as religious fervour or the world of bullfighting – are some of the most fascinating and attractive elements for foreign audiences. Today, there are many who, without knowing Spain, feel a strange closeness to the country thanks to Almodóvar's films. His vision, somewhat grotesque and disproportionate at times, is far removed from conservative circles and leans towards characters of low social status. It has been able to adapt to different periods – from glam and the Madrid *Movida* of the eighties to the social portrait and the critical sentiment of the twenty-first century – and which perfectly defines the style of the director from La Mancha. Perhaps this is why he has always refused, despite multiple offers, to set one of his films outside his own country and to work with crews and casts from other countries. Almodóvar's cinema and Spanish idiosyncrasy have been linked from the very first moment and will continue to be so until the last of his projects.

Almodóvar's tendency to exaggeration and the construction of extravagant characters has also allowed him to establish the archetype that gives meaning to his films: the strong, determined woman who manages to overcome the blows of fate and confronts the patriarchy, so present in the Spain of the Transition (the period from the mid-1970s to the early 1980s, during which Spain saw the end of Franco's regime, the introduction of democratic elections and the adoption of a new constitution) in which Almodóvar began shooting his first works. His ability to delve into such a complex female universe and extract extraordinary characters from it, as if he shares a sensibility alien to most men, is astonishing.

Born on 25 September 1949, in the small town of Calzada de Calatrava (Ciudad Real), in the heart of La Mancha, Pedro Almodóvar was accustomed from an early age to being

BELOW: Over more than four decades, Almodóvar has become one of the world's most admired filmmakers thanks to his emotionally charged, challenging and passionate vision.

“

I LEARNED A LOT FROM MY MOTHER, WITHOUT EITHER OF US BEING AWARE OF IT.

LEFT: From the beginning of his career, Almodóvar has supervised every detail of his works, from the first lines of the script to the final editing.

surrounded almost exclusively by women. His father, Antonio, was a mule driver and spent prolonged periods of time away from home, leaving Pedro and his siblings – Antonia, María Jesús and Agustín – in the care of their mother, who was always surrounded by relatives and neighbours. He, meanwhile, observed them with affection and admiration: 'They were the secret power of Spain, a kind of communal force that had managed to survive the post-war period. It is true that, in my films, the women are very strong, with enormous moral independence and full of energy. And the fact is that, although we have all grown up in a very macho society, women have managed to exercise power in silence.'

Almodóvar continued to develop this special devotion when, at the age of nine, he moved with his family to Madrigalejo, a village in Extremadura. It was there that he began to focus his gaze on the figure of his mother, Francisca Caballero, a generous and tenacious woman who, soon after arriving in their new home, set up a small business reading and writing letters for illiterate neighbours, which she adorned with marvellous embroidery. 'Sometimes, I would listen to what my mother read, and I was astonished to hear that it did not match the content of the letter,' Almodóvar remembered in 2000, during his investiture as Doctor Honoris Causa by the University of Castilla-La Mancha. 'Back home, I reproached her for inventing part of the content, and she defended herself by saying to me: "but have you seen how happy Grandma was to hear that her granddaughter remembered her?"' Over time, Francisca would become a regular presence in his films ('although she never saw any of them, because she had the intuition that she would not like them') and a continuous source of inspiration for his stories, as shown by the unforgettable Jacinta, played by Chus Lampreave in *The Flower of My Secret* (1995). 'I learned a lot from my mother, without either of us being aware of it,' he wrote after her death in 1999. 'I learned something essential to my work, the difference between fiction and reality, and how reality needs to be supplemented by fiction to make life easier.'

The women created by Almodóvar are true cinematic icons, and it is no coincidence that his best and most awarded feature films – *Women on the Verge of a Nervous Breakdown* (1988), *All About My Mother* (1999) and *Volver* (2006) – feature these charismatic fighters based on his own mother, brought to life by magnificent actors who, over the decades, have confirmed themselves as colossal muses: Carmen Maura, Cecilia Roth, Victoria Abril, Marisa Paredes, Verónica Forqué, Penélope Cruz. Even in those films in which the central character is a man, such as *Labyrinth of Passion* (1982), *Matador* (1986), *Law of Desire* (1987), *Live Flesh* (1997), *Talk to Her* (2002) or *Pain and Glory* (2019), we find female characters that in many cases sustain the emotional stability of the male protagonist, someone much weaker and unstable by nature. This is due, in the director's eyes, to the fact that women possess a gift unattainable for any man: motherhood, undoubtedly one of his most recurring themes – because the memory of Francisca will always accompany him – and a feeling capable of oscillating between happiness and tragedy, with such representative examples as *What Have I Done to Deserve This?* (1984), *High Heels* (1991) or *Julieta* (2016).

Around the powerful figure of the woman, Almodóvar began to define a series of characteristic themes that would end up defining his personality. One of the most significant is his fervent rejection of clerical authoritarianism, the result of his student years spent with Salesian and Franciscan fathers at a school in Cáceres. 'Now I can say that there were three places where I was formed: the patios of La Mancha where the women made bobbin

RIGHT: A short break during the filming of *Volver*, one of his most complex and introspective films.

lace, sang and criticised the whole town; the explosive and free-flowing nightlife of Madrid from '77 to '90, and the dark, religious education I received from the Salesians in the early sixties,' he stated in 2023 at the time of the publication of his first book of short stories.

The experience caused him to rebel and impregnate his films with criticism of ecclesiastical dogma, seen in the irreverence of *Dark Habits* (1983) or the autobiographical story of *Bad Education* (2004), in which he recalled the admiration his beautiful voice aroused among the religious or the terrible abuse suffered by some of his classmates. 'All the ceremonial was a theatrical experience that amazed me,' he confesses. 'But there came a moment when I saw that those hands holding the chalice had very recently been caressing things they shouldn't be caressing. . . At that moment I stopped having faith.' Alongside this controversial desire to confront the power of the Church, we can identify other equally important themes that have run through his work from the beginning: homosexuality and transsexuality as identity struggles, drug use as an escape route from physical and emotional pain, prostitution, and the 'cinema within the cinema', so present in *Law of Desire*, *Tie Me Up! Tie Me Down!* (1990), *Broken Embraces* (2009), *Pain and Glory* and *The Waning Lover*, the silent film included in the prologue of *Talk to Her*.

All of these themes are paraded before the camera either as drama or a comedy – and often both – the two genres that best suit his artistic vision. But while he has employed these for most of his films, there have been very successful forays into film noir during his more mature later years. In Almodóvar's films, genres never maintain their classic structure, but intermingle and enrich each other, giving rise to a unique, tragicomic and provocative brew. His lighter films always include heart-rending passages and situations, while the more dramatic works feature numerous shots of that dark humour so characteristic of his scripts. It is very likely that we will never see him directing a science fiction story or a musical, because the simple context would distort his universe.

Almodóvar has never hidden the multiple references in his films, from the more rowdy and politically incorrect John Waters of the early works to the irreverence of Billy Wilder, passing through the classic perspective of masters of melodrama such as Douglas Sirk or Howard Hawks in his most mature and relaxed stage, without forgetting the silent influence of Alfred Hitchcock – in practically all his films there is a murder or an accident that triggers the narrative – or the imprint of other great Spanish directors such as Luis Buñuel or Víctor Erice. He discovered all of them during the summers in Madrigalejo, when he and his brother, Agustín, attended the screenings that took place on the wall of an old building. 'Basically, they showed spaghetti westerns, although we also saw Bergman, Welles or Antonioni.'

During the rest of the year, while he attended his classes at the Catholic school, he repeated the ritual by escaping to a cinema in the same street: 'The priests tried to form my spirit, deforming it with religious tenacity. Engulfed in the cinema seat, I was reconciled with the world, with my world. Very soon, I was forced to choose, and I did so with that forcefulness of inexperience. If I deserved hell for watching *Johnny Guitar*, *Picnic*, *Splendor in the Grass*, and *Cat on a Hot Tin Roof*, I had no choice but to accept such a punishment. I did not know what genes were, but, without a doubt, in my genetic code I had the stigma of the provincial cinephile branded red hot.' During those sessions in Cáceres, the young Pedro discovered that films were not made by the stars, but that behind them there was

> WE CAN RECOGNISE ANY OF HIS FILMS BY A SINGLE FRAME, STUNNED BY THE VISUAL IMPACT IT PRODUCES.

a scriptwriter who shaped the story and a director who gave instructions. And he immediately knew that he wanted to do both. So, when he returned to the village after finishing his studies in Cáceres, the first thing he did was to tell his parents that he was going to Madrid to pursue his dream. His father, he recalls, 'threatened to hand me over to the National Guard,' to which he replied: 'Do it. But I'm going.'

Almodóvar's catalogue of references encompasses other arts that go beyond the cinematographic, starting with music. He typically features songs, carefully selecting ones whose lyrics always help to describe an attitude or a state of mind, and continuing with literature, through authors as diverse as Jean Cocteau, Tennessee Williams or Mary Shelley, whose *Frankenstein* must have been a fundamental book for Almodóvar while he was preparing the asphyxiating *The Skin I Live In* (2011), his triumphant reunion with Antonio Banderas after twenty-one years without working together.

On the formal side, painters such as Andy Warhol and Salvador Dalí contributed, to give personality to the palette of primary colours in Almodóvar's films, where red, the symbol of passion, always occupies a predominant place in the sets, objects, and the costumes of the characters. We can recognise any of his films by a single frame, stunned by the visual impact it produces. So important and exquisite is it for Almodóvar to maintain the identifying aesthetic in his works that he has cast Rossy de Palma – an actor of overwhelming presence and genuine figure – on seven occasions without ever having to reserve a leading role for her.

For all these reasons, and for many more that we will have the opportunity to explore, Pedro Almodóvar is a master of contemporary cinema. Even his most misunderstood films, like *Kika* (1993) or *I'm So Excited!* (2013), have those flashes of genius that are only within the reach of the chosen ones. His list of accolades is virtually unmatched: two Oscars, two Golden Globes, four BAFTAs, Best Director at the Cannes Film Festival, four César Awards, a Golden Lion in Venice, five Goyas, National Film Award, Prince of Asturias Award of the Arts, Knight of the French Legion of Honour, Doctor *honoris causa* from the Universities of Oxford and Harvard. . . To speak about Almodóvar is to speak of a creator with an indisputable international dimension, someone who has been able to maintain the essence of his art through the intimacy of stories that are close, extreme and profoundly Spanish.

An author with an infinite imagination, creator of unforgettable characters, promoter of a challenging and captivating cinema.

LEFT: During his youth, Almodóvar represented the rebellious spirit of a society awakening from the nightmare of Franco's regime.

PEPI, LUCI, BOM AND OTHER GIRLS LIKE MOM

PEPI, LUCI, BOM AND OTHER GIRLS LIKE MOM

Pepi, Luci, Bom y otras chicas del montón (1980)

In the late 1970s, a countercultural phenomenon began to take shape in Madrid. Over the following decade, the *Movida* challenged and removed the artistic constraints of a country silenced by Franco's dictatorship. Inspired by punk and new wave bands, the movement celebrated the arrival of democracy with an uncontrolled burst of creativity, which included everything from music to painting, photography, literature and fashion. Cinema, of course, was no stranger to this outpouring of freedom and provocation, consecrating such outstanding filmmakers as Fernando Colomo, Iván Zulueta and Fernando Trueba, and above them a young man from La Mancha who had arrived in Madrid at the tender age of eighteen trying to emulate his idols Federico Fellini, Ingmar Bergman and François Truffaut.

However, Pedro Almodóvar had to wait to realise his dream. The only film school in the city had closed its doors by order of Franco, who considered it a dangerous hotbed of communism. In 1969, after some sporadic jobs as a disc jockey and an extra in some movies (he always got brief roles as a hippie thanks to his looks and his characteristic long hair), he ended up getting a job as an administrative assistant at Telefónica, a position he would keep for twelve years. Despite everything, he always kept his aspirations intact and never stopped going to art and rehearsal halls. With the emergence of the *Movida*, Almodóvar became one of the most active figures in the movement: he was a member of the underground theatre group Los Goliardos; created the cult punk-glam duo Almodóvar & McNamara with Fabio McNamara; wrote short novels, newspaper stories and transgressive comics; and, despite a lack of resources, he began to make his own experimental works in Super 8 with the help of several friends.

'Super 8 was really my only school,' he confesses. 'It allowed me to touch all genres: musicals, biblical films, comedies. . . I wasn't aware of it, but those films show very clearly what I wanted to do in the cinema.' Little by little, short films such as *Dos putas o historia de amor que termina en boda* (1974), *La caída de Sódoma* (1975), *Sexo va, sexo viene* (1977) or *Salomé* (1978) consolidated Almodóvar as one of the leading figures of the Madrid phenomenon, thanks to his provocative, extreme and surrealist perspective. As none of the films had sound, during the screenings he gave for his friends, he himself was in charge of the soundtrack: 'I would stand in the middle of the audience, next to the projector, and I would do all the voices, explain, narrate the story, sing, sometimes even criticise the things I didn't like about the actors, and I had a small cassette where I would play music to accompany it.'

ABOVE: A moustachioed Almodóvar comments on a scene with Carmen Maura, the muse of his early films.

NEXT PAGE: The filmmaker soon became the creative and spiritual leader of each of his films.

In 1978, Almodóvar shot his first feature-length work, the experimental melodrama *Folle... Folle... Fólleme Tim!*, although his first commercial film did not arrive until two years later. Two friends and colleagues in Los Goliardos, Félix Rotaeta and Carmen Maura, convinced him to turn the story he had written for a photo novel entitled *Erecciones generales* (*General Erections*) – a play on words in reference to the first free elections in Spain in forty years – into a film script. 'I felt an absolute physical need to make the film,' he says. 'I really liked the script. But, as I didn't have any resources, I had to improvise the production.' Rotaeta and Almodóvar's generous friends raised the necessary funds – around half a million pesetas – to make *Pepi, Luci, Bom and Other Girls Like Mom* an unforgettable calling card for a filmmaker swimming against the tide, revealing the first daring brushstrokes of his art in which sex, masochism and even a mythical golden shower scene filmed with hot beer and an enema douche are all present.

Depicting the director – gender swapped – in practically all his early works, Carmen Maura plays Pepi, a young woman who grows cannabis on her terrace and who, in exchange for her silence, is raped by her policeman neighbour (Félix Rotaeta). Seeking revenge, Pepi meets Luci (Eva Siva), her attacker's wife and an extreme fan of pain, who pushes her

“SUPER 8 WAS REALLY MY ONLY SCHOOL.”

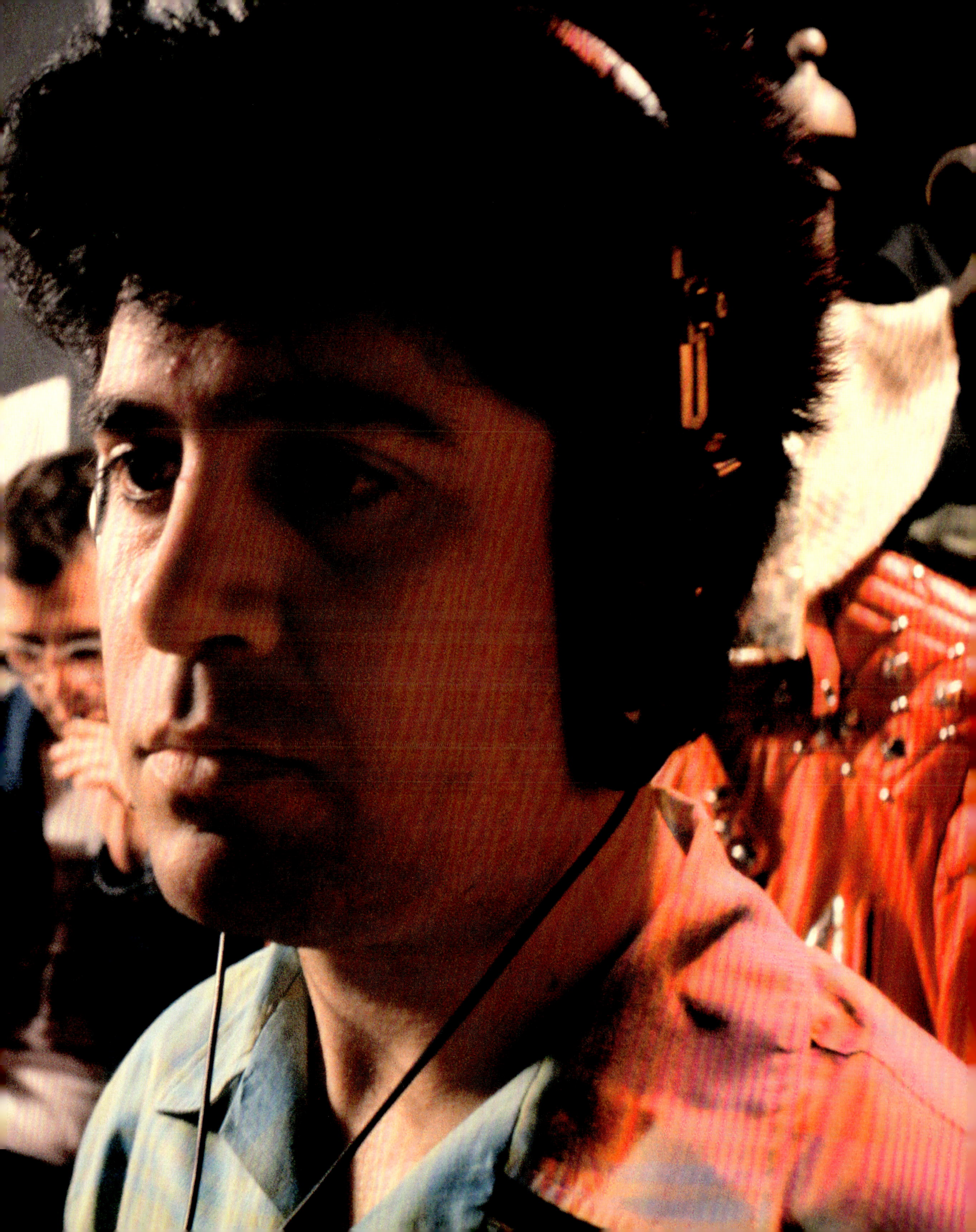

into the arms of Bom (played by the singer Alaska, another of the undisputed icons of the *Movida*), a cursed punk artist with sadistic tendencies. The three women are just the spearhead of a gallery of bizarre and fascinating female characters, some of them played by key actors from Almodóvar's later films, such as Julieta Serrano, Kiti Mánver and Cecilia Roth.

LUCI: **What do you do for a living?**
PEPI: **Well, I'm a rich heiress and my parents give me money, but they've had enough, and they've told me to get by as best I can.**
LUCI: **And what are you going to do now?**
PEPI: **Well, I thought I'd start by selling my virginity, but the other day I was raped, and my plan was ruined.**

The scarcity of means and the meagre budget led to an endless and creative shoot. Production began in 1979 and had to be suspended on several occasions due to lack of money, not being completed until almost a year-and-a-half later. During this time, the crew alternated exhausting fifteen-hour filming days with long months without work, which meant that some roles had to be changed and actors replaced, as some were not available. The actors were responsible for providing their own wardrobe and often did each other's make-up, always ready in case the director called them to shoot a scene the following day. As if all this were not enough, Almodóvar had to combine the film with his work at Telefónica – he could only devote his full

"I REALLY LIKED THE SCRIPT. BUT, AS I DIDN'T HAVE ANY RESOURCES, I HAD TO IMPROVISE THE PRODUCTION."

LEFT: Almodóvar reviews the script with his actresses and adjusts Eva Siva's hair before shooting.

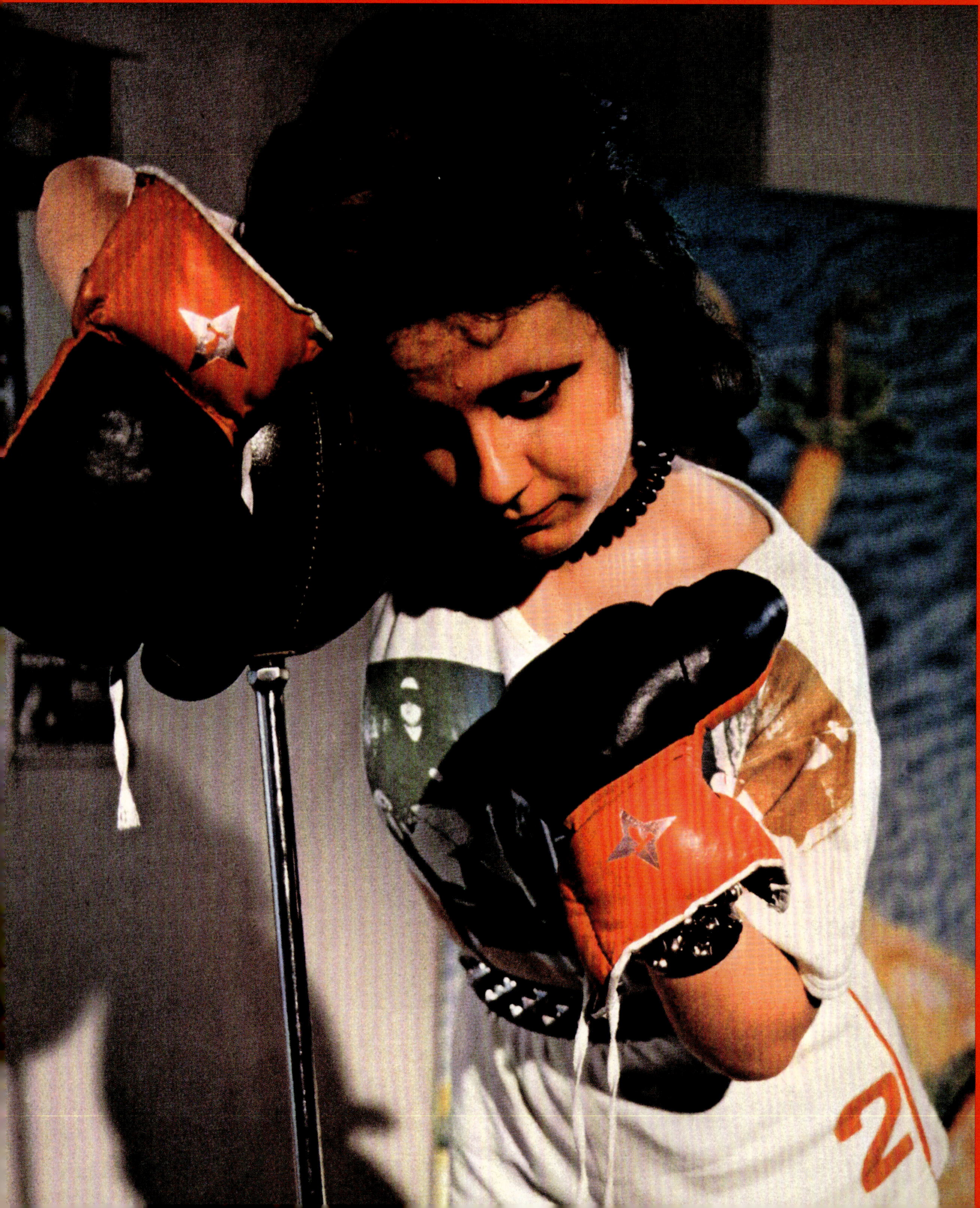

> WHEN A FILM HAS ONLY ONE OR TWO FLAWS, IT IS CONSIDERED IMPERFECT, WHEREAS WHEN THE DEFECTS ARE SO PROFUSE, THEY CONSTITUTE A STYLE.

LEFT: Singer Alaska, one of the outstanding icons of the Movida, was only sixteen when she played Bom.

attention to it at weekends – and make sure he completed the exterior sequences in the shortest possible time, as they lacked permits to shoot on public roads.

There was even a moment when the director, tired of so many delays, thought of shooting a hasty ending and truncating the length of the film: 'At the beginning, Pepi opens the door to the policeman in June 1979, he sits in the living room in December of that same year and starts talking in June 1980,' Almodóvar himself would admit years later, and his main concern was 'to reach the *end* word.' Everything changed when the producer Pepón Coromina saw the material they had shot and decided to provide distribution advances in order to finish the film, which was completed with a final budget of around six million pesetas and was even presented out of competition at the San Sebastián Film Festival: 'I had to continually adapt to the lack of resources, which meant I had to give up some scenes and also meant that I could not replace fragments of the material shot at the beginning with scenes that, a year later, seemed more appropriate.'

Finally, on 27 October 1980, the film premiered at the legendary Alphaville cinema in Madrid, where it practically became a night-time emblem of the *Movida* and remained a midnight showing mainstay for almost four years, reaching a final box-office taking of close to forty million pesetas. Shortly before, Almodóvar had been able to fill the Carrión Theatre during the Valladolid Film Festival, after personally putting up posters all over the city with the slogan of his debut film. 'It's full of defects,' he acknowledged, while at the same time claiming the existence of his own spirit based on those same singularities. 'When a film has only one or two flaws, it is considered imperfect, whereas when the defects are so profuse, they constitute a style. That's what I jokingly said when I was promoting it, but I think it's pretty close to the truth. We made it with two coins, on handouts, passion, and unconsciousness, but I approached it as seriously as if I were shooting *Gone with the Wind*.'

It is paradoxical that, four decades later, a story like *Pepi, Luci, Bom and Other Girls Like Mom* is inconceivable in the current industry. The carefree vision of some particularly tricky subjects, the irresistible amateur aesthetics, and the firm commitment to incorrectness make it a rarity in which some of its creator's fundamental themes begin to be glimpsed. We can find the attraction to the female universe – with those stoic and charming women, the perfect counterweight to the clichés of toxic masculinity – or the representation of sex and passion in its freest and most diverse version, without limits or rules. A work impossible to classify, where the genres are confused and cinema is shown in its purest state, as a glorious explosion of creativity and bravery.

LABYRINTH OF PASSION

LABYRINTH OF PASSION

Laberinto de pasiones (1982)

ABOVE: Fabio McNamara, half of the legendary musical duo Almodóvar & McNamara, was one of the most charismatic and uncontrollable presences on-set.

The nightly pilgrimage of viewers to the Alphaville cinema to see *Pepi, Luci, Bom and Other Girls Like Mom* led its managing director, Javier de Garcillán, to design a budget plan with which to finance Pedro Almodóvar's second feature film. He himself decided to contribute seventy per cent of the twenty million pesetas that the film would cost, raising the rest through various private contributions. Aware of the complexity of the script and the numerous technical shortcomings of the director's previous film, Garcillán was determined to assemble a first-rate team, including the director of photography Ángel Luis Fernández – a benchmark of the period thanks to his contribution to such iconic works as *Ópera prima* and *Arrebato* – and the German Martin Müller, the regular sound designer for Wim Wenders's films. All of this was done with the intention of elevating the Almodóvarian gaze to a new formal and narrative dimension, much closer to professional cinema than the irregular – although captivating – *Pepi, Luci, Bom*. The filmmaker himself acknowledged that he was overcome by a clear aspiration: 'To say that it is a delicious and unclassifiable comedy is not enough, I know. But I can talk about my intentions. Well, here they are: my only intention with this film is to conquer the world, and by the way, to move house, to broaden the horizons of my private life and to convince myself that life is worth living.'

Labyrinth of Passion was not only filmed at the height of the *Movida*, but also represents the filmmaker's most complete homage to the spirit of that unrepeatable era. Its story full of subplots and its wide gallery of characters – no less than fifty – is directly reminiscent of the choral and sophisticated comedies directed by masters such as Billy Wilder or Richard Lester, two influences recognised by Almodóvar himself. 'I've always felt very close to the genre of delirious comedy,' acknowledges the director. 'When I wrote the script, my desire was to show that Madrid was the first city in the world, a

“MY ONLY INTENTION WITH THIS FILM IS TO CONQUER THE WORLD, AND BY THE WAY, TO MOVE HOUSE.”

LEFT: Almodóvar, who was thirty-two years old when the film was released, was already one of the most transgressive and admired artists of the emerging Spanish countercultural movement.

ABOVE: Cecilia Roth as the volcanic Sexilia, her first leading role under Almodóvar's direction.

place where all kinds of people came and where anything could happen. In fact, there was a version that featured Dalí and the Pope, who met there and had a great love story. This passage was deleted from the film, but it sums up its ironic nature very well.' Beyond these influences, *Labyrinth of Passion* is, above all, a wayward taboo-free version of the drama *Luna* (Bernardo Bertulocci, 1979), the harrowing story of a successful singer whose teenage son plunges into the world of drugs when he feels abandoned by his mother.

Almodóvar chose two young performers with barely any experience in front of the camera to play the main characters, and they later became big names in the industry. The Argentinian Cecilia Roth, established as a muse of the *Movida* thanks to her appearances in *Arrebato* and *Pepi, Luci, Bom and Other Girls Like Mom*, would play Sexilia, a singer with a wild personality who has sex with men compulsively to overcome a childhood trauma related to her father, a well-known gynaecologist who has developed a revolutionary fertility method. For his part, Imanol Arias would assume his first leading role as Riza Niro, an Arab prince who arrives in the city in search of new experiences after the fall of the despotic regime of his father, the Emperor of Tiran. Both will live a strange and passionate

love story in which they will have to face the different obstacles that prevent them from achieving happiness.

As he did in his first film, Almodóvar completed the cast with names as varied as the German actor Helga Liné, who plays the mother of the wayward prince (which was the director's first exploration of the maternal–filial conflict so characteristic of his later work). Also noteworthy are the performances of the excellent Marta Fernández Muro and a very young Antonio Banderas in his film debut, portraying a terrorist who tries to kidnap Riza and ends up falling madly in love with him. Alongside them is the presence of important musical figures from the *Movida*. The film is above all a pop celebration of its extravagant and legendary underground artists and bands, from the members of Radio Futura, transmuted here into an emblematic group of Madrid partygoers, to the confrontational Fabio McNamara, so undisciplined during the filming that he had to be directed from inside the

ABOVE: The German actress Helga Liné had already appeared in more than a hundred films when she joined the cast.

shot, as he never remembered the marks and continually went off-camera. According to Almodóvar, 'Fabio has a very strong personality, so I directed him almost like an animal, in a very shocking and violent way. But, at the same time, I allowed him much more freedom than the other actors because what I wanted to get from him was the expression of his own character. Since I couldn't control him from behind the camera, I got inside the frame to tell him exactly the things he had to say and to keep him tied up.'

Almodóvar asked Telefónica for an unpaid leave of absence to shoot the film, which was produced between March and April 1982. On its tour of Madrid, *Labyrinth of Passion* visits venues closely linked to the artistic life of the time – and by extension to Almodóvar's – such as La Bobia, Tablada 25 and Sala Carolina, and draws on compositions by artists such as Alaska y los Pegamoides and Bernardo Bonezzi, known as 'the Mozart of the Movida', a precocious and unconventional genius who was barely eighteen years old when the film was shot. The author himself would admit that, beyond its classic boy-meets-girl approach, the film is a compendium of love stories that gravitate around urban music and opposing gangs, with obvious references to *West Side Story* (Robert Wise and Jerome Robbins, 1961) and *Quadrophenia* (Franc Roddam, 1979).

With *Labyrinth of Passion*, Almodóvar also inaugurates a very particular plot universe, in which the stories and characters from his different works appear connected in a particularly subtle and witty way. On this occasion, the self-referential figure is the star of porn novels Patty Diphusa, a sort of female alter ego that the filmmaker created in the early eighties on behalf of the art publication *La Luna*, and who is here quoted in an article in the magazine that Riza Niro leafs through. Her wild spirit would give rise over the years to a novel and even a theatrical adaptation in Mexico City, as well as being very present in titles of pure debauchery such as *I'm So Excited!*

Many critics received the film with some dismay. They were very curious to see Almodóvar's new work after *Pepi, Luci, Bom and Other Girls Like Mom*, which was quite acclaimed at the time. However, they found a frenzy of eccentric characters, multiple narrative lines and an exaltation of subjects that were still taboo for Spanish cinema, such as drugs or sexual freedom in all its expressions. Even Almodóvar himself has admitted on occasion that he was not prepared for a challenge of this magnitude, although the film, despite the lack of enthusiasm for it after the premiere has emerged as a brilliant and beautiful evocation of the freedom of the years of the *Movida*. The public adored it unreservedly: an audience of almost 400,000 and ten years of late-night screenings at the Alphaville attest to this.

"I'VE ALWAYS FELT VERY CLOSE TO THE GENRE OF DELIRIOUS COMEDY."

DARK HABITS

DARK HABITS

Entre tinieblas (1983)

With his first two films, Pedro Almodóvar had shaken the artistic foundations of a country silenced for decades by dictatorship. Artists' yearning for freedom during the transition to democracy demanded a defiance towards everything established, including, of course, scrupulous respect for Catholicism. It was only a matter of time before such an unusual filmmaker decided to tackle the moral degradation hidden behind the doctrines of Francoism, although in his case it would be from an even more subversive perspective, using the crudest satire and parody. *Dark Habits* is, once again, the result of the riotous creativity of the *Movida*, 'a crazy, playful period, full of feverish nights, where Madrid was an explosion that left the world speechless,' as described by Almodóvar when the film was revived in 1996. 'That was the turbulent world to which I belonged, I don't understand where I found the time, but apart from going to Rock-Ola every night and getting high on substances, I was still working at Telefónica, shooting movies and singing.'

Although *Pepi, Luci, Bom and Other Girls Like Mom* and *Labyrinth of Passion* had received some curious financing, *Dark Habits* managed to get off the ground in an even more unusual way. Producer Luis Calvo was looking for a project to satisfy the ambitions of his wife, Cristina Sánchez Pascual, an actor of modest ability who was desperate to work with one of her three favourite Spanish directors: Luis García Berlanga, Iván Zulueta and Pedro Almodóvar. Determined to fulfil her wish, Calvo contacted each director and offered to finance any script if his wife could play the lead. Almodóvar, aware of the difficulties of starting a project about a drug addict and lesbian nuns, ended up being the most astute of the three and accepted the proposal, ahead of an indecisive Berlanga.

LEFT: With *Dark Habits*, Almodóvar turned his biting and provocative gaze on religion for the first time.

A CRAZY, PLAYFUL PERIOD, FULL OF FEVERISH NIGHTS, WHERE MADRID WAS AN EXPLOSION THAT LEFT THE WORLD SPEECHLESS.

ABOVE: Almodóvar's main inspiration for creating the troubled artist was Marlene Dietrich's films of the 1930s.

Almodóvar had conceived *Dark Habits* as a drama about a powerful female character, a bolero singer who seeks refuge in a convent after the death of her boyfriend from a drug overdose. His main inspiration was the films directed by Josef von Sternberg in the 1930s starring Marlene Dietrich, in which the German actor gave fascinating performances thanks to the effect of her close-ups. However, after witnessing during rehearsals the acting limitations of the lead imposed on him, he decided to strengthen the film's comic component and divert the viewer's attention to the group of nuns who make up the community of the 'Humiliated Redeemers'. These include the Mother Superior, addicted to heroin and determined to give shelter to troubled young women with whom she ends up falling in love; Sister Damned, a cleanliness obsessive who takes care of the tiger that the nuns keep as a pet, feeding it and entertaining it with the bongos; Sister Manure, a fan of LSD and sadomasochism; and Sister Sewer Rat, a secretive nun who leads a double life as the author of pornographic bestsellers.

For these roles, Almodóvar chose, respectively, Julieta Serrano (whose career had been built playing in great theatrical dramas, and who almost turned down the offer because she did not trust her comedic skills), Carmen Maura, Marisa Paredes and Chus Lampreave,

and thanks to their combined talents, he discovered the possibilities and power of close-ups, which he considered 'a kind of X-ray of the character, because they offer no room for lying.' Leaving aside his inseparable Maura, this group of actors would become core cast members in many of Almodóvar's later films, especially Lampreave, who would appear in seven more until her death in 2016. 'He had already called me for his first film, and then for *Labyrinth of Passion*,' she said. 'But I didn't work because I was scared, I didn't feel like making movies. Then he kept insisting and told me that he would always call me with every new film, and he has done so.'

Sister Sewer Rat is probably the great revelation of *Dark Habits*. Almodóvar creates a character to match Lampreave's comic skill and gives her the most memorable lines; when the nun receives a visit from her sister Antonia (Eva Siva), who secretly publishes her novels and brings her literary magazines to the convent:

SISTER SEWER RAT: **Did you bring it?**

ANTONIA: **Yes, there's a review inside.**

SISTER SEWER RAT: **And what does it say?**

ANTONIA: **Not much. What did you expect? An article by Umbral?**

(Passing the magazine slyly under her habit)

ANTONIA: **Do you have any ideas? They're waiting for something new.**

SISTER SEWER RAT: **We're going through a bad time, you know. A new girl has come in, but I don't think it will solve anything. I don't know what's wrong with me, but sometimes I've thought about leaving all this and starting afresh.**

ANTONIA: **What are you saying? It's too late to change your life. Your place is here. Besides, where are you going to go when you're forty-eight years old?**

SISTER SEWER RAT: **Hey, no! Forty-seven, if you don't mind [. . .] Times have changed a lot, life isn't the same anymore.**

ANTONIA: **Come on, look. . . Those are nun's fantasies. You're all crazy, because, as you don't set foot on the street, you think that things happen in the street. Nothing happens in the street! Everything, everything, everything is exactly the same as when you came here.**

SISTER SEWER RAT: **Why?**

ANTONIA: **Because I'm telling you, I live outside, and I know!**

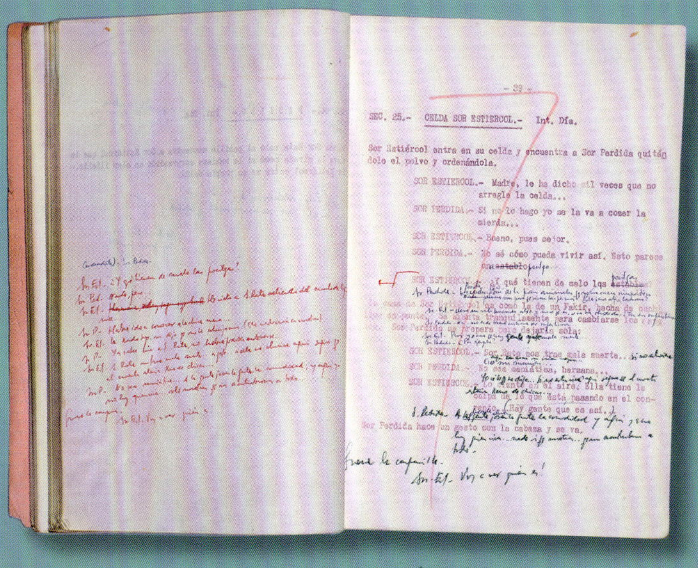

OPPOSITE and TOP: Mercedes (Cecilia Roth) the cabaret singer begs Mother Superior (Julieta Serrano) for forgiveness.

ABOVE: *Dark Habits* original script, with annotations and corrections by the director.

> IT WAS THE FIRST FILM IN WHICH I BEGAN TO BECOME AWARE OF THE LANGUAGE, OF THE MEANING OF THE SHOTS.

ABOVE and LEFT: In *Dark Habits*, Almodóvar cast three of the most important actresses of his career: Julieta Serrano and Marisa Paredes (above), and Chus Lampreave (left with the filmmaker).

'It was a continuous joy to watch these four nuns work,' Almodóvar admits. 'The mixture of Chus, Carmen, Julieta and Marisa was marvellous. . . It was a shoot worth remembering, for that reason and because I have never again been more scared while filming one of my films.' The scare he refers to occurred when, before filming the confession scene, the tiger attacked a wardrobe assistant and bit her leg. 'It was stuffed with food, so it didn't tear the leg, but it took several crew members to open its mouth and free the girl.' Practically the entire film was shot in an old convent in Madrid, Santa María Magdalena, located at number 88 Hortaleza Street. Shortly afterwards, the building was acquired by the UGT trade union to house its new headquarters, although they soon decided to abandon it, claiming that it was haunted.

With *Dark Habits*, Almodóvar refined and built on the style of his previous films: formal splendour, marginal characters in search of redemption, and a refined direction of his performers. We also find an almost perfect fusion between the melodrama of Douglas Sirk or Rainer W. Fassbinder and the unbridled comedy of John Waters, sprinkled with the irreverent anticlericalism of Luis Buñuel's works such as *Viridiana* (1961) or *La Voie lactée* (1969). All of this was wrapped up in magnificent and unbridled provocation, still strange for a country in the midst of reconstruction, which, by tackling religious hypocrisy, laid the foundations for future projects, such as *Bad Education*, with the Church as the target. 'It was the first film in which I began to become aware of the language, of the meaning of the shots, of the significance of each shoot's size,' he says of his leap in maturity. 'I suppose that, having a unique scenario, a unique set, forced me to think a lot more about where to place the camera so as not to repeat myself.'

Dark Habits marked the beginning of Almodóvar's international recognition, although its controversial approach almost prevented it from being screened at the Venice Film Festival, the first foreign event he attended, on the recommendation of the Italian writer and critic – as well as a regular collaborator of Bernardo Bertolucci – Enzo Ungari. The festival director, Gian Luigi Rondi, opposed the film's inclusion in the official section as he branded it 'obscene,' but he could not prevent it from being screened out of competition, where it received one of the most enthusiastic and unexpected ovations of that year. The audience was delighted with its daring and sense of humour, and reviews in the press, such as *Corriere della sera*, described Almodóvar as 'the heir to Pier Paolo Pasolini,' while others referred to him as the 'Mediterranean Fassbinder.'

The film arrived in Spanish cinemas in October 1983 to mixed reviews from critics but public acclaim, while in France it attracted an audience of 54,000 in its first week of release. The influential Spanish newspaper *Diario 16* declared it 'the scandalous film of the year,' highlighting that 'its central story is that of a love affair between a heroin-addict convent superior and a whoremongering slut who ignores her completely.' Although many consider it the most rushed and least personal film of the director's early work, *Dark Habits* has become recognised as a significant cult piece of art, to the extent of being part of an exhibition at the Reina Sofía Museum in Madrid between 2018 and 2020.

WHAT HAVE I DONE TO DESERVE THIS?

ABOVE: Carmen Maura (right), accompanied here by a splendid Verónica Forqué (left), turned Gloria into one of her most long-suffering and celebrated characters.

WHAT HAVE I DONE TO DESERVE THIS?

¿Qué he hecho yo para merecer esto!! (1984)

Encouraged by the strong box-office performance of *Dark Habits*, Luis Calvo wanted to produce Almodóvar's next film. *What Have I Done to Deserve This?*, the film that marks the end of Almodóvar's early career, introduces some key themes of what is to come: frenzy and surrealism give way to a more mature portrait of the failures of post-Franco Spanish society, while the storytelling is tempered by a much more meticulous *mise-en-scène*. All this is done without giving up the usual flashes of black comedy or the gallery of over-the top characters, each with their own quirks and traumas. The result was a work of early maturity that, even today, is among the director's best works.

The screenplay of *What Have I Done to Deserve This?* is partially based on *Lamb to the Slaughter*, a 1953 short story by British novelist Roald Dahl, popularised five years later by Alfred Hitchcock in his TV series *Alfred Hitchcock Presents* – it was one of the few episodes that the master of suspense directed himself. In it, a housewife who is devoted to her family murders her husband with a frozen leg of lamb, which she later ends up serving as dinner to the police officers investigating the case. Based on this premise – in the film, the lamb would be replaced by *jamón* – Almodóvar depicts the squalid life of Gloria (the amazing Carmen Maura), a woman addicted to amphetamines, who works as a cleaner and dedicates all her time to supporting her dysfunctional family. This gaudy group consists of her taxi driver husband, Antonio, her ungrateful mother-in-law, two children – one a drug dealer and the other in love with his best friend's father – and even a lizard they call Dinero (Money). Her only friend is her neighbour, Cristal, a naive and kind-hearted sex worker whose friendship keeps Gloria going.

Thanks to its extraordinary depiction of social reality in Spain in the mid-1980s, *What Have I Done to Deserve This?* is the Almodóvar film that comes closest to the raw, poignant and hopeful spirit of Italian neorealism. 'The critics started talking about me as a director because I was dealing with the tribulations of a poor housewife, and you could tell that my heart was very close to this character,' he said. 'And I, who was a very modern guy, very night owlish and all that, had no shame in saying that this is the social class I belong to. That neighbourhood and that building where the protagonist lives contain all the characters that are dear and familiar to me. In my cinema I move around clichés, by prototypes, I digest them and express them in my own way, but in the background, there is the Neorealism of Vittorio de Sica with Sophia Loren or Anna Magnani screaming, dishevelled. . . That's why I thought that this was my Italian film par excellence.' However, there is a distinction that sets Almodóvar

apart from movements such as the postwar period in Italy or the Nouvelle Vague: 'They took the cameras out onto the streets because they wanted to film life honestly. And they achieved all the possible semblance of truth because cinema, including documentary, is full of tricks. I love both periods and they have produced dozens of masterpieces, but what interests me most about reality is its representation. I'm not interested in showing it as it is.'

Gloria is one of those Almodóvarian women who turns to legal drugs to escape their frustrations, loneliness and depressing lives. In one of the film's most memorable scenes, Gloria reveals her total anguish when she goes to the pharmacy – a recurring place for the director from a tragicomic perspective – in search of medicines to help her alleviate her despair:

PHARMACIST: **What do you want?**
GLORIA: **Good evening. I'd like Minilip.**
PHARMACIST: **That's not available without a prescription. Besides, it's been withdrawn.**
GLORIA: **Give me Bustaid then.**
PHARMACIST: **We have neither.**
GLORIA: **Well, they've always given it to me without a prescription!**
PHARMACIST: **Well, that's too bad.**
GLORIA: **Well, give me. . . Dexedrines, or something similar. . . I'm very nervous.**
PHARMACIST: **You must have the syndrome.**
GLORIA: **Syndrome? And what is that?**
PHARMACIST: **Look, madam. Go to the doctor, tell him you're a drug addict and have him write you a prescription.**
GLORIA: **I'm a drug addict? But. . . You're insulting me!**
PHARMACIST: **Ma'am, all you're asking me for is drugs.**
GLORIA: **Well, well. . . Well, I'm a drug addict. Drug addict! And what do you want me to do? Assault you and take you by force, or what?**
PHARMACIST: **I've already told you what the rules are.**
GLORIA: **And what are the rules when you must work all day and you can't keep your soul?**

Although the role of Gloria continues to be one of the professional highlights of Carmen Maura's career, Almodóvar found it hard to convince himself that she was the right actor for the part. 'He wanted a tougher woman,' the Madrid-born artist would admit years later. At the time, she had established herself as one of the great progressive voices of the post-Franco culture, thanks to the talk show she presented on Spanish television, *Esta noche*. Almodóvar thought it would be difficult for the audience to accept her as a cleaner on the verge of despair so had decided to offer the role first to two other veteran actors, Esperanza Roy and Concha Velasco, both of whom turned it down. His hand forced, the director went back to Maura, who returned his trust by giving one of the best performances of Spanish cinema in the eighties.

ABOVE: The film's cast included two renowned Spanish directors: Gonzalo Suárez (with Almodóvar, right) and Jaime Chávarri.

Almodóvar assembled a stellar cast of acting talent, both new and experienced, around his leading lady. On the one hand, he demonstrated his great intuition when casting new

FERRETERIA

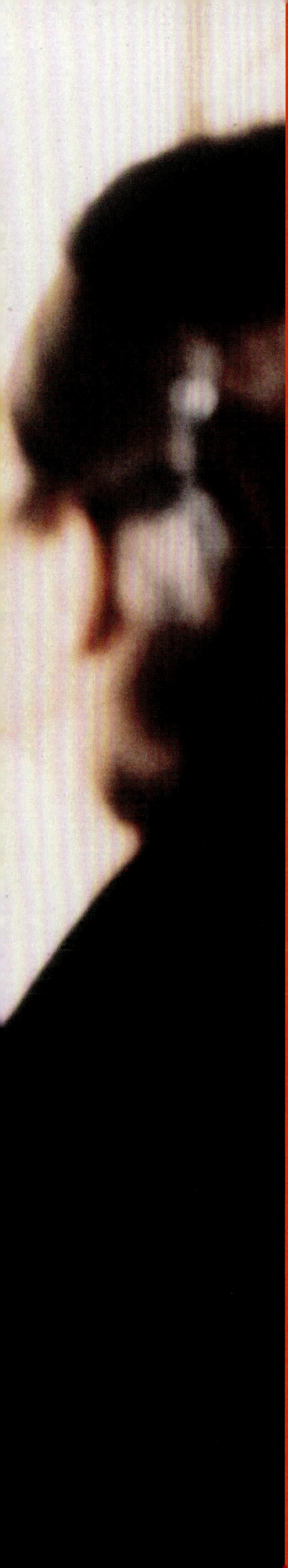

“WHAT INTERESTS ME MOST ABOUT REALITY IS ITS REPRESENTATION. I’M NOT INTERESTED IN SHOWING IT AS IT IS.”

performers such as Ángel de Andrés López and the dazzling Verónica Forqué, whom he would collaborate with again in *Women on the Verge of a Nervous Breakdown* and *Kika*, respectively, while also relying on faces that were already regulars in his films, such as Kiti Mánver or Chus Lampreave, the latter's role as the Grandmother being the first of her many irreverent Almodóvarian matriarchs. Even his own mother, Francisca Caballero, appeared briefly in a clear reference to the role of motherhood and its different interpretations at play in the story. 'The film is a parade of monsters, a reflection on the institution of the family. I get on very well with my family, although I have put some distance between myself and them... I think that the family unit is very good for a society that tries to control and repress the individual,' Almodóvar declared.

Filming took place during the first months of 1984, in such symbolic locations as the Barrio de la Concepción in Madrid, a neighbourhood located next to the M-30 highway which, at that time, was home to the famous 'beehive buildings' where poor families from different parts of Spain lived on top of each other. However, most of the film was shot in a studio, where the flat in which Gloria lives with her family was recreated, and where Almodóvar shows a maturity unbecoming of a director with only three films to his credit. The use of the almost poetic fixed camera shots – another legacy of the neorealist masters – is splendid and captures the range of emotions of each character as they move between the pathetic and the sublime. 'The film is like the reverse of the comedies of Doris Day and Rock Hudson, in which the world of the home became a paradise where household appliances made them very happy,' the director says of the importance of the space in which most of the story takes place. 'Here, on the other hand, the fridges are dwarfed, they have almost no light and when you open them all you find is a can of out-of-date *sofrito*.'

The film received excellent reviews and was a notable success with audiences in Spain. It also became Almodóvar's first work to be commercially released in the United States. After the initial impact of the Venice screening of *Dark Habits*, *What Have I Done to Deserve This?* opened the doors of international cinema and announced him, in the eyes of the American press, as one of the most important European filmmakers of the time. *Los Angeles Weekly* defined his style as a perfect blend of Buñuel, Waters and Woody Allen, and *The New York Times* stated that the film was 'a wonderful black comedy, simply a small masterpiece.' But the strongest validation came from *Newsweek* magazine: 'After nearly fifty years of repression, the arts are finally reviving in Spain... A cultural renaissance the country has not seen since Picasso and Buñuel left for Paris at the turn of the century.' The world was beginning to take notice of Almodóvar, to revel in his unusual and exuberant cinema, as he prepared an unpredictable move and would succumb, once again, to the influence of his masters.

PREVIOUS PAGE: After the film, Maura and Forqué worked together again in various projects and developed a long and close friendship.

LEFT: Lucas Villalba (Suárez) and his wife Patricia (Amparo Soler Leal) hatch a plan to get money from his brother.

RIGHT: Chus Lampreave, here as the Grandmother, would become the quintessential Almodóvarian mother figure.

MATADOR

MATADOR (1986)

Spanish cinema has always been a magnificent exponent of European noir. In recent decades, directors such as Enrique Urbizu (*No Rest for the Wicked*, 2011), Mariano Barroso (*Washington Wolves*, 1999), Agustín Díaz Yanes (*Nobody Will Speak of Us When We're Dead*, 1995) and Alberto Rodríguez (*Marshland*, 2014) have lifted the genre to another level in Spain, though curiously, the contribution of Pedro Almodóvar tends to be overlooked. No one doubts that his work usually follows other narrative paths, although the criminal component has always played a leading role in his stories, not only in those films with a purer structure (*Live Flesh* and *The Skin I Live In*), but also in others framed as comedy or drama, such as *Women on the Verge of a Nervous Breakdown*, *Kika*, *Volver*, *Broken Embraces* or, as we have just seen, *What Have I Done to Deserve This?* Not surprisingly, Almodóvar has always been a lover of film noir, never hiding the fact that several of his favourite films are classics of the genre, such as *Night of the Hunter* (Charles Laughton, 1955), *Out of the Past* (Jacques Tourneur, 1947) or *Touch of Evil* (Orson Welles, 1958), to cite just a few examples.

With *Matador*, Almodóvar began a new artistic phase in which he opted for a greater formal perfectionism and for stories where sex and death are closely linked. Initially, the story was about a director in his twilight years who agrees to shoot a musical for the greater glory of a dwarf actor, whose closest friend is a murderer with multiple personalities. 'I started to feel more interested in that character than in the other two, so I decided that the script would revolve around him,' he said of this first foray into the world of erotic noir, starring two characters who find a morbid source of pleasure in the suffering of others. Diego (Nacho Martínez) is a retired bullfighter with a sexual fixation for slasher films, and whose obsession with death leads him to murder the women he makes love to. Meanwhile, María (Assumpta Serna) is a young lawyer who defends political prisoners and shares Diego's fondness for killing each of her lovers after sex. When the two meet, they begin a love-hate relationship that will inevitably bring tragic consequences.

The title of *Matador* was chosen by Almodóvar not only because it was short – *What Have I Done to Deserve This?* was so long that it was difficult to fit onto the promotional posters – but it was also a word that did not need to be translated internationally. '*Matador* contained the whole essence of the story because it refers to someone who kills, and this is a circumstance that affects the two protagonists. . . it's not a film about bullfighting,' Almodóvar said in 1986. 'It's about a character who is physiologically linked to death, and how that determines all his romantic relationships, especially the one he has with the lawyer played by Assumpta Serna. One is the bull and the other the bullfighter, and then they swap roles. In the film, bullfighting allows me to talk about pleasure, physical pleasure, and the relationship of both with death.'

In the mid-1980s, Serna was one of the most promising actors in the country after working with such prestigious filmmakers as Pilar Miró, Carlos Saura, Mario Camus and

BELOW: Almodóvar chose Assumpta Serna after Charo López and Ana Belén turned down the role of María.

> *MATADOR* CONTAINED THE WHOLE ESSENCE OF THE STORY BECAUSE IT REFERS TO SOMEONE WHO KILLS . . . IT'S NOT A FILM ABOUT BULLFIGHTING.

LEFT: Nacho Martínez had a 'bullfighting bearing' that made him perfect for the role of Diego.

Bigas Luna, and Almodóvar opted for her after being turned down by Charo López, first, and Ana Belén, later. Nacho Martínez had already appeared in *Tasio* (1984) and *Extramuros* (1985) and secured the role mainly because of his moody aura and his 'bullfighting bearing.' Almodóvar once again assembled a solid cast in which Antonio Banderas stood out, playing a young man from a well-to-do background, a student at the bullfighting school, who plunges into a spiral of confusion when he confesses to the police to the murders perpetrated by Diego. Alongside him, other important Almodóvarian figures stand out in secondary roles, such as Carmen Maura, Eusebio Poncela, Julieta Serrano and the already essential Chus Lampreave, transformed again into a stoic mother, Francisca Caballero's alter ego.

Almodóvar had by now become the visible head of a generation of filmmakers who symbolised freedom and artistic abundance, someone who, moreover, was beginning to shine at major international events. This allowed him to tackle *Matador* with an infrastructure far removed from the chaotic and unsophisticated filming of his early years. The budget of 120 million pesetas was supplemented with a grant from the Spanish Ministry of Culture and the support of Andrés Vicente Gómez, by then considered one of the most respected and prolific producers in the industry thanks to his collaborations with filmmakers of the calibre of Gonzalo Suárez, Fernando Trueba and Orson Welles. 'It is the first time that the Ministry has offered a film of mine a grant without stinginess,' said Almodóvar on a controversial issue, which even required the publication of an open letter by the Insituto Nacional de Cinematogafia y de las Artes Visuales (ICAA). 'Despite the fact that they like my films, more or less, they have verified that they are admired abroad and have given me the category of a cultural export. I think this is the most aggressive of my films, and if the others scared them, this one will scare them even more, so they must know they are subsidising my radicalism.'

After setting out to make a film full of brutal crimes in the style of *The Texas Chainsaw Massacre* (Tobe Hooper, 1974), Almodóvar opted instead to make a film that was 'elegant and exquisite, where violence was replaced by emotions and feelings.' In this sense, it is worth highlighting the magnificent cinematography by

“I THINK THIS IS THE MOST AGGRESSIVE OF MY FILMS, AND IF THE OTHERS SCARED THEM, THIS ONE WILL SCARE THEM EVEN MORE.”

RIGHT: Actress Eva Cobo points a (fake) gun directly at the camera during a break in filming.

Ángel Luis Fernández based on a series of visual recommendations from Almodóvar. These included the melodramas of Douglas Sirk, the works of the Golden Age painter Francisco de Zurbarán, and the captivating Technicolor of the classic *Pandora and the Flying Dutchman* (Albert Lewin, 1951).

Surprisingly, audiences and critics did not embrace the change of direction that *Matador* represented. Despite its gripping plot and hypnotic *mise-en-scène*, the film was widely misunderstood at the time and was the first artistic setback for its director. At the first Goya Awards – created to recognise the best work in Spanish cinema – the film received only one nomination, in the supporting actor category (Antonio Banderas), and was ignored in the rest. As is usual in these cases, and especially in Almodóvar's work, *Matador* gained fans over time and has become one of his most loved pieces. One of these fans, Quentin Tarantino, has acknowledged that it was one of the films that encouraged him to become a filmmaker: 'That opening scene… There was nothing like it available in America. I thought I wanted to do shit like that, to always shoot whatever I wanted to do, and thanks to that we managed to change the cinema of the nineties.'

LEFT: *Matador* marked the second collaboration between Almodóvar and Antonio Banderas, four years after *Labyrinth of Passion*.

RIGHT: The relationship between Diego and Maria is inevitably scarred by perversion and death.

“I THOUGHT I WANTED TO DO SHIT LIKE THAT, TO ALWAYS SHOOT WHATEVER I WANTED TO DO.”

LAW OF DESIRE

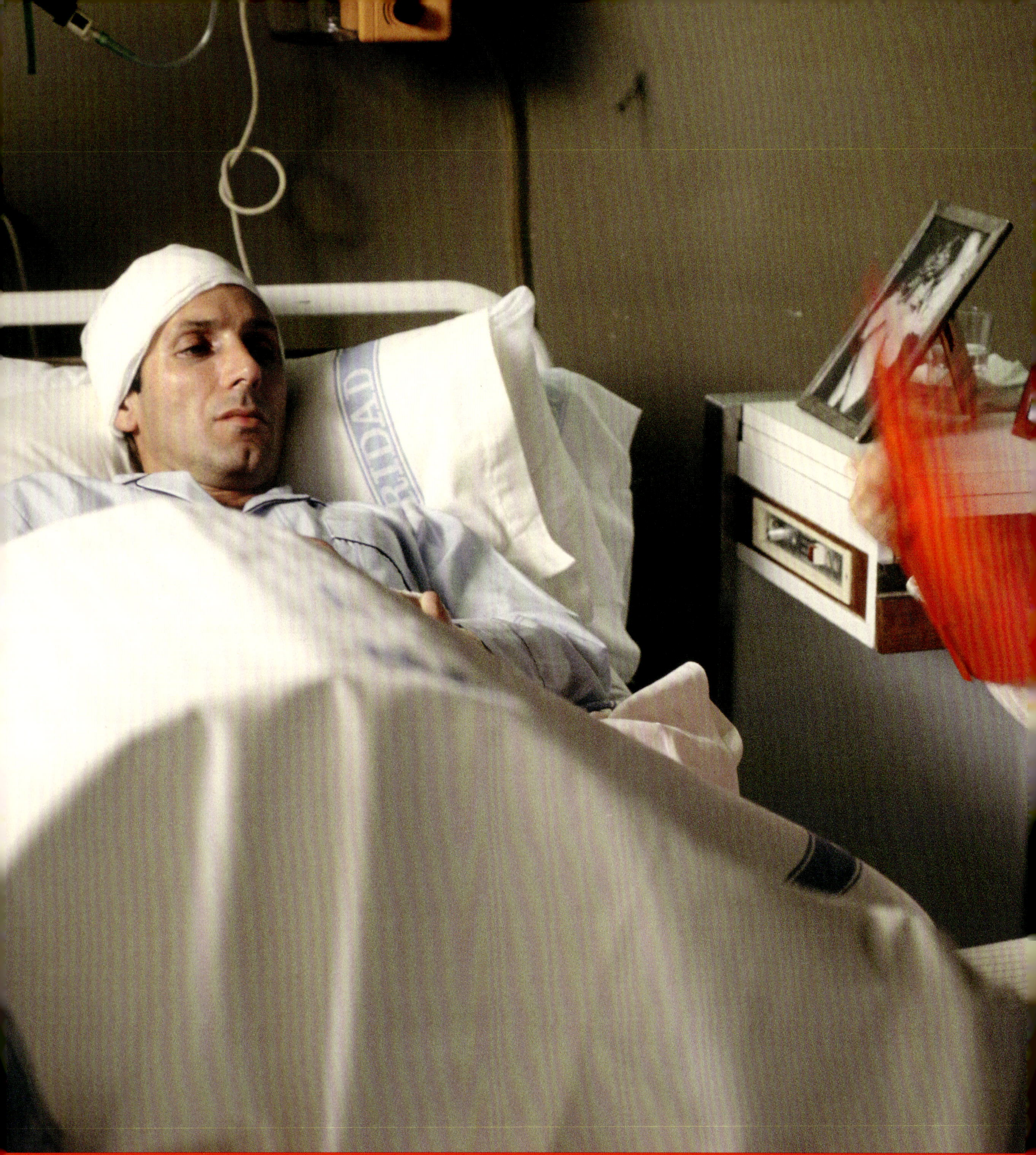

LAW OF DESIRE

La ley del deseo (1987)

While Pedro Almodóvar became one of the great figureheads of the cultural vibrancy of Madrid in the 1980s, his younger brother, Agustín, graduated in Chemistry and initially chose a profession in a very different area. However, fate, together with Pedro's bad experiences with the producers of his early films, would have the two brothers founding one of the most important production companies in contemporary Spanish cinema. Established at the beginning of 1986, El Deseo (Desire) was born of Almodóvar's need to control his works as much as possible, conveying to the public his uniquely personal vision untainted by the commercial interests of an external funder. One of the greatest privileges he gained from doing so would be to shoot his scripts in chronological order, a process that, at great expense, considerably enriches the actors' performances and that, even today, is within the reach of very few filmmakers.

'I have been lucky, because being a boy of my type, and in an industry like this, I have been able to make a film a year, jumping from one producer to another,' he recognised at the time. 'But there's something about me that doesn't work with them. . . I felt like I had five children with five different fathers, and I was always arguing with

> IT'S A TRIBUTE, I ADORE HIM, AND I ALWAYS WANTED TO MAKE A FILM ABOUT BROTHERS.

them over custody. Producers are capable of all kinds of atrocities with negatives, and I wanted to be able to decide for myself. We were gambling everything; it was an all or nothing bet. But I believed in that film, and I took all the risks. That's why it is so fundamental in my career.' The film to which Almodóvar refers is *Law of Desire* – hence the name of the company – and it featured the first appearance of one of the recurrent alter egos in his career: the figure of a filmmaker, to be seen again in *Broken Embraces* and *Pain and Glory*. 'It was as if I were starting all over again, as if I were shooting my first film and it was about a character very close to me, who works in the same profession.'

That character is Pablo Quintero (the charismatic and elegant Eusebio Poncela), a successful film and theatre director who is in love with Juan (Miguel Molina), a much younger man who does not reciprocate with the same intensity, and whom Pablo will replace, fleetingly, with the attractive Antonio (Antonio Banderas) who is obsessive and potentially dangerous. Pablo is very close to his sister Tina (Carmen Maura), a transsexual actor who is dedicated to raising her ex-lover's daughter.

It seems far from coincidental that this brotherly bond is at the heart of the first film produced by El Deseo, as if Almodóvar wanted to vindicate the driving force that two brothers can generate; in fact, the name of Tina comes from *Tinín*, a diminutive Pedro uses to refer to Agustín. 'It's a tribute, I adore him, and I always wanted to make a film about brothers.'

Pablo and Tina, like the Almodóvars, share an artistic bond that sometimes leads to confrontations typical of two disillusioned and wounded people still searching for their place in the world.

PABLO: **As you're a bit paranoid, before you read it, I want to warn you so that you don't get upset.**

TINA: **What's going on? What's the script about?**

PABLO: **Do you see? You're already upset.**

TINA: **Tell me now, otherwise I'll get really upset.**

PABLO: **[. . .] Look, you see. . . Your role. . . It's not that it's inspired by you, but it has a certain affinity. . .**

TINA: **How much of an affinity?**

PABLO: **Well, when it comes to your problems with guys.**

TINA: **I don't have problems with guys, because for me they haven't existed for a long time.**

PABLO: **And that doesn't seem like much of a problem to you?**

TINA: **What's the matter? Are you going to treat me like I'm a freak too?**

PABLO: **Stop. . . I didn't say that.**

TINA: **Talk about your own problems with guys and leave me alone [. . .] I forbid you to discuss even the smallest details of my life! As ridiculous as it is, I have the right to be respected!**

PABLO: **But who said your life is ridiculous?**

TINA: **I don't need anyone to tell me. I know that [. . .] My failures with men are more than just the plot of a script. I won't allow you or anyone else to play with them!**

PREVIOUS PAGE: In one of his most personal films, Almodóvar pays tribute to his brother Agustín and to overcoming adversity with fraternal support.

ABOVE: In *The Law of Desire*, Almodóvar broke with all genre conventions to create a work totally ahead of its time.

The family, the gravitational axis without which it would be impossible to understand Almodóvar's cinema, is represented in his early films in a totally unusual way, challenging and dismantling all the patriarchal clichés imposed by the dictatorship. Although in his films from the nineties onwards they began to acquire a more classical structure, in the eighties the Almodóvarian families break away from traditional concepts and become a place of refuge for marginalised characters who seek – and need – to feel loved. Blood ties between parents and children are so flawed that they sometimes lead to traumatic episodes that drag on forever, and the family ends up being a matter of complicity and affinity, of a love built on acceptance. In *Pepi, Luci, Bom and Other Girls Like Mom*, the three protagonists establish a union with which to face – and lean against – the world, while in *What Have I Done to Deserve This?* the traditional family is so grotesque and suffocating that the closest thing to a *sister* that Gloria has in her life is her sex worker neighbour. In *Law of Desire*, Pablo, Tina and little Ada (Manuela Velasco) end up forming their own nucleus, one in which the role of father figure is occupied by a gay artist and the maternal figure by his transsexual sister. Undoubtedly, this is complex and dense terrain for any director, but Almodóvar navigates through it with mastery.

ILFORD

Law of Desire was filmed in Madrid during the sweltering summer of 1986. Almodóvar knew how to take advantage of the deserted and rundown appearance of the city during the holidays, offering the viewer an urban portrait of a place where the *Movida* was in its last throes and the bohemian atmosphere was about to succumb to the invasion of big business. 'The film is a complete celebration of Madrid, and more specifically of Madrid in the eighties. It was like *La La Land*, a city where dreams come true, at least for me. I remember how quickly and easily it was shot. Everything was light and simple, and there was an incredible rapport with the crew. A kind of miracle where everything happened in a harmonious and natural way. We did not stop laughing, it is something that is stuck in my memory.'

Especially distinctive was the moment, totally improvised, in which Tina asks a man who is washing down the streets with a hose to 'water' her as well. 'I asked Carmen if she minded if we watered her, because it is a wish that I have always had on hot nights in Madrid. The city hall employee who was holding the hose was freaked out, but he loved watering Carmen Maura.' The most curious thing was that, at first, the actor fell to the ground due to the force of the water, and she had to be taken to a nearby bar to dry her hair and make-up before filming again. 'It is a moment that for me identifies and represents the whole film, because, under that spontaneous watering, the character suddenly becomes an explosive image of desire.' Years later, the writer Susan Sontag – one of the cultural figures most admired by Almodóvar – would tell him that the powerful imagery of the scene was comparable to that of Marilyn Monroe's raised skirt in *The Seven Year Itch* (Billy Wilder, 1955).

Law of Desire became a key title for contemporary melodrama after its release. The frankness with which Almodóvar portrayed homosexuality within the framework of a tragic romance, at a time when not even *The New York Times* used the word *gay*, was nothing short of revolutionary, and even today its boldness and ability to build characters so full of life, passion and dreams is still surprising. It was recognised with the Teddy Award for best LGBT feature film at the Berlin Film Festival and won several other international awards, although in France its poster was censored because it showed two naked men in bed together. Sadly, but not surprisingly, it was ignored and at the Goya Awards, an omission that particularly annoyed Almodóvar, and precipitated his love-hate relationship with the awards: 'It hurt me, because at that time we did need a little support. But that absence didn't hurt me for me, but for my team. That Carmen and Antonio were not nominated seemed flagrant to me. It was a full-fledged grievance.'

> "EVERYTHING WAS LIGHT AND SIMPLE. A KIND OF MIRACLE WHERE EVERYTHING HAPPENED IN A HARMONIOUS AND NATURAL WAY."

PREVIOUS PAGE: A thoughtful and exhausted Almodóvar during a brief break in filming.

RIGHT: At the age of 23, Rossy de Palma was cast in the first of her eight films with Almodóvar.

WOMEN ON THE VERGE OF A NERVOUS BREAKDOWN

WOMEN ON THE VERGE OF A NERVOUS BREAKDOWN

Mujeres al borde de un ataque de nervios (1988)

In one of the most iconic scenes from *Law of Desire*, Carmen Maura's character, Tina, performs an excerpt from *The Human Voice*, the acclaimed 1930 play by Jean Cocteau about a woman who, abandoned by her lover, waits impatiently for a phone call to end her despair. Almodóvar had always had a fascination with Cocteau's monologue and conceived that moment in the film as his tribute. However, Maura's superb performance soon made him decide that he had to adapt the whole piece just for her.

Almodóvar's initial intention was to make a small, experimental film with a modest budget, and just the actor in front of the camera. However, when he realised that the text of *The Human Voice* was not long enough for a feature film, the filmmaker opted to reinvent the play's theme of abandonment and focus on the forty-eight hours prior to it, moving from a story with a single character to a festive parade of extravagant women and unreliable men. Many were surprised by this turn by the director, moving away from his usual agitating and daredevil cinema towards the sophisticated comedies of the fifties: 'The characters don't take drugs, they don't drink, they don't even smoke because the doctor advises against it. They don't have time to do dirty things either. It is my reunion with immaculate comedy,' he said shortly after filming commenced. *Women on the*

ABOVE: Lucía (Julieta Serrano) threatens Pepa (Carmen Maura) while she holds a glass of the famous gazpacho.

“THE CHARACTERS DON’T TAKE DRUGS, THEY DON’T DRINK, THEY DON’T EVEN SMOKE BECAUSE THE DOCTOR ADVISES AGAINST IT.”

RED ALWAYS APPEARS . . . IN SPANISH CULTURE, IT IS ALSO THE COLOUR OF PASSION, BLOOD AND FIRE.

PREVIOUS PAGE: Marisa (Rossy de Palma) will be one of the first to be affected by the cocktail of sleeping pills.

LEFT: Almodóvar shows Carmen Maura how to spike the gazpacho with sleeping pills.

Verge of a Nervous Breakdown would become a landmark film for Almodóvar, launching his international commercial career and confirming, in the eyes of the world, his status as a genuine artist.

In fact, Almodóvar's core themes were still very much present (female camaraderie versus male violence, unhealthy relationships, conflicts between parents and children) but this time from a completely light-hearted and derisive perspective. 'I didn't want to do something boring, quite the opposite,' he explained. 'You can tell the story of a woman torn apart by grief without having to frighten the audience as if the theatre was shaken by an earthquake. I had to find a way to make that pain recognizable, identifiable, and work like a magnet. Everything was going to depend on the tone, so I decided that high comedy was the most appropriate.' Almodóvar discarded the dramatic component and the structure of *The Human Voice*, but he would return to Cocteau's universe, showing a much more tragic abandonment in *The Flower of My Secret*, first, and turning the original piece into a short film, later. In this way, *Women on the Verge of a Nervous Breakdown* was nourished by the influence of masters such as Lubitsch, Sturges, Hawks, Wilder and even Hitchcock and *Rear Window* (1954), as it progressively became a crazed reflection on such complex themes as loneliness and lack of communication (that omnipresent telephone that never rings, a wink from the director to his years at Telefónica). The result is a wonderful tangle that turns suffering into laughter, and despair into hope.

Pepa (Carmen Maura) works as a dubbing actor, as does her lover, Iván (Fernando Guillén), a playboy who uses women and then abandons them. 'When thinking about *The Human Voice*, I suddenly came up with a natural medium, and that is that they were both dubbing actors,' explained the filmmaker. When Pepa discovers she is pregnant, Iván breaks off the relationship and disappears without a trace, leaving only an answering machine message asking her to put his things in a suitcase. She, who still dreams that Iván will reconsider his decision, rents out the penthouse they shared because she cannot bear to continue living there alone, and a parade of bizarre characters begins to populate the house: Iván's ex, who has just left the psychiatric hospital; their son Carlos and his girlfriend; Pepa's best friend, Candela, who is hiding from the police because her boyfriend is a terrorist. . . Almodóvar achieves in all of them a perfect cocktail of fun and pathos, as the women who arrive at the apartment are united by an anguish that makes them as vulnerable as they are reckless.

LEFT: As in *Dark Habits*, Julieta Serrano's character Lucía embodies the most genuine Almodóvarian humour.

PEPA: **Where is Ivan?**

CARLOS: **Well. . . I don't know.**

PEPA: **Why doesn't he call me? I must talk to him.**

CARLOS: **I don't see him much, you know?**

PEPA: **Don't lie to me too. He's going on a trip with your mother.**

CARLOS: **With my mother? No way! But she thinks he's going with you!**

PEPA: **So, he's going with someone else? Of course. . . That's why he didn't spend the night in the studio.**

CARLOS: **And how can you be so sure?**

PEPA: **Because I've been up all night going from your house to the studio, and from the studio to your house. You'll think I'm crazy. . .**

CARLOS: **A bit nervous. . . But it's normal if you haven't slept. . .**

PEPA: **. . . At all.**

CARLOS: **Ivan never told you he had a son?**

PEPA: **Never. I had no idea. With your father it's impossible to know anything! I always find out everything by chance. Like last night. I was in the cabin, the suitcase fell, it opened, a portrait of you came out with a dedication: 'From your father, Ivan, who doesn't deserve you.' And that's how I found out. He never says anything. He never acknowledges anything. Not even a reproach comes out of his mouth.**

The cast, with the addition of Almodóvarian depth in Julieta Serrano, Antonio Banderas, Kiti Mánver and a hilarious Chus Lampreave, is simply unbeatable. Special mention should be made of two actors who significantly contributed to magnifying the film's mythology: Rossy de Palma, whose distinctive profile would become the most potent expression of the director's universe in another six films, and María Barranco, who was chosen for the role of Candela ahead of the original choice – Victoria Abril – just as the actor was considering leaving the profession due to a lack of opportunities (the director found her so nervous and overwhelmed during filming that he ordered her to clean the set 'so that she could blow off steam'). With all of them, and with Carmen Maura at the peak of her career, Almodóvar locked himself in a studio to shoot the bulk of the film in a set built for the occasion, although the address of the attic did correspond to a real place in Madrid: number 7 Montalbán Street.

Pepa's apartment perfectly represents in miniature Almodóvar's own obsessions, peculiarities and whims. From the flamenco dolls to the rubber flowers, the chicken coop, the deckchairs or the beach ball, all the elements seem out of place but, at the same time, are in perfect harmony with the surreal setting in which the story unfolds. The whole is saturated in red: Pepa's dress, the telephone, the *gazpacho* laced with sleeping pills, common in all of Almodóvar's work and especially visible here. 'Red always appears, but I don't know why,' he said. 'However, an explanation can be found. Red, in Chinese culture, is the colour of those condemned to death, which makes it a human colour. But, in Spanish culture, it is also the colour of passion, blood and fire.'

Since *Pepi, Luci, Bom and Other Girls Like Mom*, Almodóvar's films had enjoyed the support and complicity of the audience, but nothing compared to the critical and commercial noise generated by *Women on the Verge of a Nervous Breakdown* when it was released in March

1988. In Spain, it played in theatres for more than a year and was seen by 3.3 million people, with a final box office of 912 million pesetas. It also won five Goya Awards that, until now, had been elusive, receiving nominations in all categories and winning Best Film, Lead Actress (Carmen Maura), Supporting Actress (María Barranco), Original Screenplay and Editing.

Success was not just limited to Spain and Europe, though Cannes refused to accept it in its official section, considering it too commercial. It was chosen to open the New York Film Festival ahead of *The Last Temptation of Christ* (Martin Scorsese, 1988), where there were ten standing ovations from the audience during the screening. It was an enormous success in France and grossed over seven million dollars in the United States, an extraordinary figure for the time for a foreign production. It was nominated for Best Foreign Language Film at the Golden Globe, BAFTA and Academy Awards, marking Almodóvar's first encounters with the academies that, in the future, would recognise the global legacy of his work with statuettes in 1999 and 2002.

Sadly, while the film achieved commercial success, and garnered widespread critical and industry acclaim, a disagreement at the Oscars between Almodóvar and Carmen Maura, blamed on the wear and tear of their professional relationship and heated clashes during filming, saw their working relationship end for a decade. 'There are consequences of the intense work that I do with the actors,' he acknowledged. 'The relationship with Carmen stopped being strictly professional and that hurt both of us.' Decades after its premiere, the characters in *Women on the Verge of a Nervous Breakdown* have become icons of popular culture, revered by an audience that embraced their misfortunes and knew how to laugh at them by throwing their phone out of the window.

ABOVE: The film brings together one of the most brilliant casts of Almodóvar's career. Candela (María Barranco) and Carlos (Antonio Banderas) drink the gazpacho under the watchful eyes of Pepa and the flamboyant Lucía.

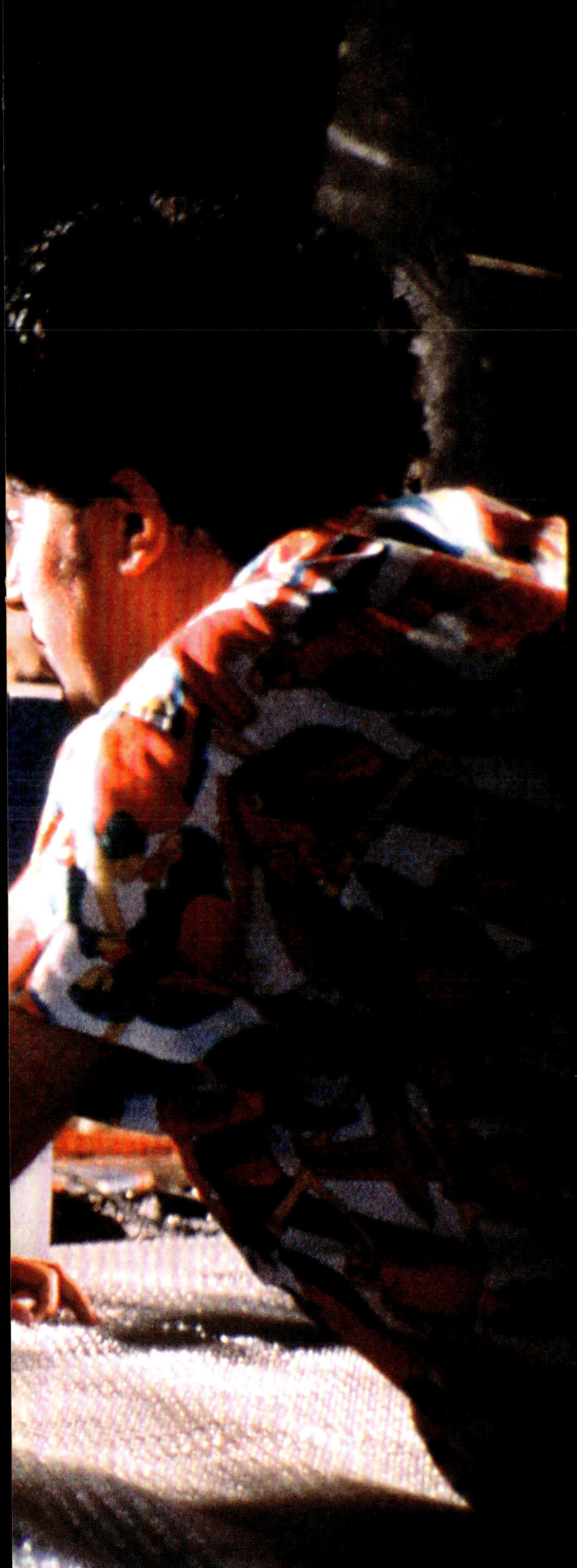

TIE ME UP! TIE ME DOWN!

TIE ME UP! TIE ME DOWN!

¡Átame! (1990)

The idea for *Tie Me Up! Tie Me Down!* began to take shape during the filming of *Women on the Verge of a Nervous Breakdown*. In that excessive and deliberately artificial location, Almodóvar imagined a second story that would take place on a film set, which would give him the freedom to include in the shot all the paraphernalia that usually surrounds studio work: cameras, technical equipment, props. . . The intention, shared with his brother, Agustín, was to shoot two films almost consecutively on a single stage, spreading their budget resources and giving the production a 'Roger Corman' feel. The story would focus on three men who have escaped from a psychiatric hospital and hide on the set of a B-movie that is about to celebrate its end-of-filming wrap party. During it, they are mistaken for crew members until they decide to take the cast and crew hostage and ask the Ministry of Culture for an unlikely ransom. Meanwhile, one of them falls madly in love with the film's female lead actor, who also begins to develop a strange attraction to her captor.

Ultimately, the enormous demands of completing *Women on the Verge of a Nervous Breakdown* caused Almodóvar to discard this initial concept, although the love story that emerges from a kidnapping would remain at the heart of the eventual film. The new approach, reminiscent of *The Desperate Hours* (William Wyler, 1955) and Luis Buñuel's classic *El ángel exterminador* (1962), follows Ricki, a young orphan who has spent several years in a mental institution. When he is discharged, he begins to stalk Marina, a former actor and recovering drug addict with whom he is obsessed, until one day he

LEFT: The film presents an interpretation of Stockholm Syndrome from Almodóvar's unique perspective.

breaks into her apartment and kidnaps her with the hope that she will eventually fall in love with him. The victim's initial reluctance gradually gives way to an unsuspected tenderness towards Ricki, when he ends up badly injured after being beaten by some drug dealers. In the end, the two run away in pursuit of a life together with Marina's sister Lola, giving rise to another of Almodóvar's typically strong and bizarre families.

RICKI: **(*Shortly after kidnapping Marina in her apartment*) I tried to talk to you, but you wouldn't let me. I had to kidnap you so that you could get to know me. I'm sure you'll fall in love with me then, as I am with you (*She looks at him incredulously*) I'm twenty-three years old and I have 50,000 pesetas, and I'm alone in the world. I'll try to be a good husband to you and a good father to your children.**

MARINA: **Are you the one who stole from the set?**

RICKI: **Yes [. . .] We met each other before. A year ago, in a bar called Lulú. Don't you remember? I had just escaped from the mental hospital. I met you by chance. Then we went to your apartment and had sex. You really don't remember? I promised I'd get you off the street and protect you.**

MARINA: **A lot of men have promised me that!**

RICKI: **But I've come back to prove it to you!**

Ricki was the first character that the director wrote expressly for Antonio Banderas, and the first leading role for the actor from Malaga in an Almodóvar film after his four earlier supporting roles. Banderas was by now one of the great stars of Spanish cinema and about to make the leap to Hollywood with *The Mambo Kings* (Arne Glimcher, 1992). Victoria Abril had already had a long and successful career in Spain and France – between 1986 and 1991 she earned six consecutive Goya nominations as Lead Actress – and had been on the verge of working with Almodóvar on several occasions, which made her the ideal performer for the character of Marina. Aided by terrific performances, and with a stellar cast featuring Loles León, María Barranco and an immense Paco Rabal, who stood out in a sort of tribute to John Huston, Almodóvar delivers a film of overflowing imagination, in contrast to the struggles of *Women on the Verge of a Nervous Breakdown*. *Tie Me Up! Tie Me Down!* marked a return to the marginal and outsider characters of his early works, and to the defining elements of his storytelling: drugs, sex, brotherly complicity, strong women and film within film. 'It is a real love story, in which we shamelessly talk about the need we all have for someone to love us,' he declared at the premiere. '*Tie me up* is the equivalent of saying I love you, with all that it entails, all that part of relationships that we are not willing to accept but that we accept because we do not want to, nor can we, live without love.'

The film was shot over three months in Madrid and the town of Granadilla, in Cáceres, where the splendid denouement takes place. For both stars, *Tie Me Up! Tim Me Down!* was to be one of the most intense and demanding experiences of their careers, especially for Victoria Abril, who spent a good part of the shoot with her mouth covered and had to be able to convey her emotions with just her eyes; for this reason, Almodóvar considers her to be the actor who cries best on screen. As if this were not enough, the adhesive tape gave her cold sores, a situation that forced the director to improvise the comical scene in the

LEFT: For his next project after *Women on the Verge of a Nervous Breakdown*, Almodóvar chose a much darker and more unnerving story.

IT IS A REAL LOVE STORY, IN WHICH WE SHAMELESSLY TALK ABOUT THE NEED WE ALL HAVE FOR SOMEONE TO LOVE US.

RIGHT: The excellent chemistry between Victoria Abril and Antonio Banderas was key to achieving the credibility demanded by the plot.

pharmacy. 'Victoria wasn't used to improvising so much on set,' said the director. 'She told me that she was not used to directors asking her for so many new things on the spot [. . .] Until she understood that she did not have to invent anything, but that I was going to invent everything for her and that what she needed was enormous flexibility to pick up everything that I suggested.' For Antonio Banderas, the sex scene was one of the most difficult to shoot, taking several hours and nine takes to complete because Almodóvar demanded the characters be tired and drenched in sweat; legendary filmmaker Elia Kazan said it was the best sex scene he had ever seen.

Tie Me Up! Tie Me Down! was Almodóvar's first film since *Labyrinth of Passion* not to feature a soundtrack by Bernardo Bonezzi. Instead, Almodóvar turned to one of the foremost composers in the history of cinema, Ennio Morricone, who at that time was enjoying one of his best creative periods thanks to titles such as *The Mission* (Roland Joffé, 1986), *The Untouchables* (Brian De Palma, 1987) and *Cinema Paradiso* (Giuseppe Tornatore, 1988). However, the relationship between the two artists was never smooth and their ways of working ended up being less than compatible. 'He had a method that didn't work for me,'

A FILM AS AUDACIOUS AS *TIE ME UP! TIE ME DOWN!*, WITH SUCH A CONTROVERSIAL PLOT, WOULD BE ALMOST IMPOSSIBLE TO MAKE IN THE FEBRILE, POLITICALLY CORRECT AND INTOLERANT WORLD OF TODAY.

LEFT: The iconic sex scene surprised even such major filmmakers as Elia Kazan, and was one of many that earned the film a NC-17 rating in the USA.

Almodóvar explained. 'I participate a lot in the music of my films, which is an essential element of the narrative. But Ennio would take the script, compose the soundtrack, and then give it to you in its entirety, and it is impossible for a first version of the soundtrack to seem totally valid to me. In the film, I kept what fitted for me, and what did not fit for me was left out. The music was much more conventional than the plot of the film [. . .] I listened to other themes of his and I realized that he did nothing but repeat himself: the central theme of Roman Polanski's *Frantic* was practically the same as that of *Tie Me Up! Tie Me Down!*' Morricone, wanting to keep all soundtrack royalties for himself, wouldn't agree to the inclusion of the Dúo Dinámico version of the song 'Resistiré'. After featuring in the film, it became a hymn to perseverance: 'I don't think he wanted to share the copyright, and that made me like him less.' Of course, the two geniuses never worked together again.

There is no doubt that a film as audacious as *Tie Me Up! Tie Me Down!*, with such a controversial plot, would be almost impossible to make in the febrile, politically correct and intolerant world of today. Even upon its release, Almodóvar had to deal with the wrath of feminist journalists at the Berlin Film Festival and with an incomprehensible X rating in the United States by the MPAA (Motion Picture Association of America), due to the infamous scene in which Marina masturbates in the bathtub with the help of a toy submarine (despite, or maybe because of, the controversy, the film grossed four million dollars at the North American box office). In Spain, both the audience and critics received it with relative enthusiasm, mainly because the huge success of *Women on the Verge of a Nervous Breakdown* had set an impossibly high bar. The film left no one indifferent and even set a record at the Goyas by failing to win any of its fifteen nominations, another sign of Almodóvar's tense and complex relationship with his homeland's most important awards.

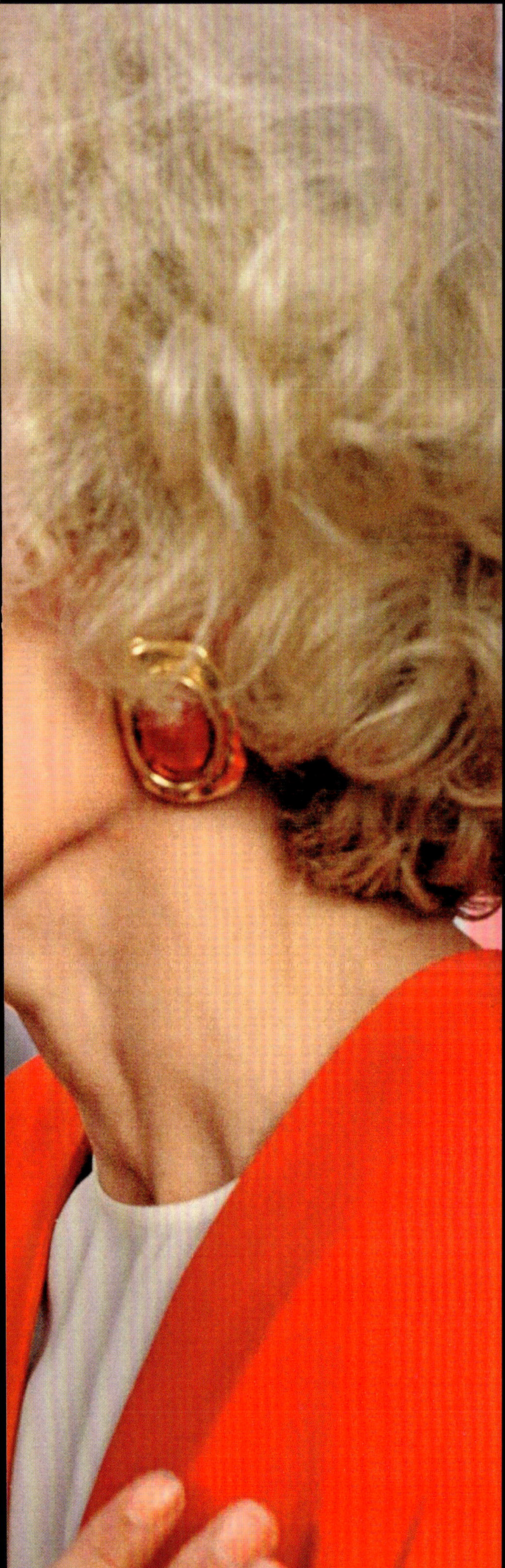

HIGH HEELS

HIGH HEELS

Tacones lejanos (1991)

Like many other Almodóvar feature films, *High Heels* was conceived as a very different work from the one we all know today. The director himself has acknowledged that many of his best ideas come to him during the long sessions prior to shooting, as a way of escaping the anxious – and at times tedious – pre-production process. While he was preparing *Tie Me Up! Tie Me Down!*, a particularly powerful image began to take shape in his mind: a television presenter confesses to a murder in the middle of a live broadcast – the death of her husband and owner of the network, no less – and then collapses in front of the cameras, showing viewers a series of photographs of his clothes, his desk – their memories together – that she had taken after his death to fight her anguish. 'I was having a coffee near my house, and at that moment the light bulb went on. I dropped everything and went upstairs to start writing straight away,' he said.

The premise seized Almodóvar, who soon had a script ready to turn his idea into a short film that he would direct once he finished *Tie Me Up! Tie Me Down!* However, the presenter further aroused his curiosity, to the point of imagining all the events and reasons that preceded the television revelation, as well as its consequences. 'She was too big a character for such a short story,' he admitted. 'So, I started developing her story from both ends, leaving the confession right in the middle. And it wasn't easy, because I wanted the character to be neither a monster nor a psychopath. My intention was for the audience to be excited by her, to come to understand her without judging or sentencing. For a simple reason of length, the narrative of a short allows you to show the facts without the need to explain or get involved in them, but a feature film needs the author to provide a detailed description of the facts to find their place within the story. And I found mine at the beginning, very close to Rebeca. That was the main difficulty of writing, directing and performing this story:

LEFT: Contrasting emotions testifying before the judge, from the strained body language between Rebeca (Victoria Abril) and Becky (Marisa Paredes), to the naivety of Isabel (Miriam Diaz-Aroca).

not to make her a nasty killer, but an angry and wounded human being, the victim of her own fear.' Victoria Abril's extraordinary work in *Tie Me Up! Tie Me Down!*, where she played a character of enormous emotional complexity, made her the ideal actor for the role of this news anchor who is trapped by her past.

The director went so far into Rebeca Giner's backstory that he ended up finding in her childhood the reason for her deep unhappiness. While still very young, her mother, the well-known singer Becky del Páramo (a sublime Marisa Paredes), abandoned her to go to Mexico in search of fame and fortune. As a consequence, Rebeca feels an overwhelming need to recover the love and lost time, but she also hides a terrible resentment for being forced to live in the shadow of the myth.

BECKY: **Why did you do it?**
REBECA: **I didn't kill him, Mom.**
BECKY: **But you confessed it yourself. Nobody made you do it.**
REBECA: **Killing him would have been the legitimate thing to do. . . But since you wouldn't even let me do that, my only revenge was to confess it, even if it was a lie!**
BECKY: **Why are you tormenting me, Rebeca, for having slept with him? Is that why?**
REBECA: **Don't be silly, you weren't the only one [. . .] I've spent my life imitating you. Ever since we separated, I've tried to compete with you in everything. And without any success. Only once have I managed to beat you! Once! With Manuel!**
BECKY: **With Manuel we both lost.**
REBECA: **Yes, but it was me who married him, not you. But you had to come here to prove to me that you could take him away from me if you wanted to. I knew it, but you had to prove it to me!**
BECKY: **Forgive me, Rebeca. I know I've been very bad to you, but what can I do now?**
REBECA: **Now you can just listen to me.**
BECKY: **You tell me.**
REBECA: **Since I was little, I was only ever a nuisance to you. But, despite my insignificance, I tried hard to be useful to you. Because I adored you [. . .] I only wanted you to be in control of your life, and you promised me that we would enjoy it together, that we would never be separated. But you didn't keep your promise. And I don't think I'll ever forgive you for that.**

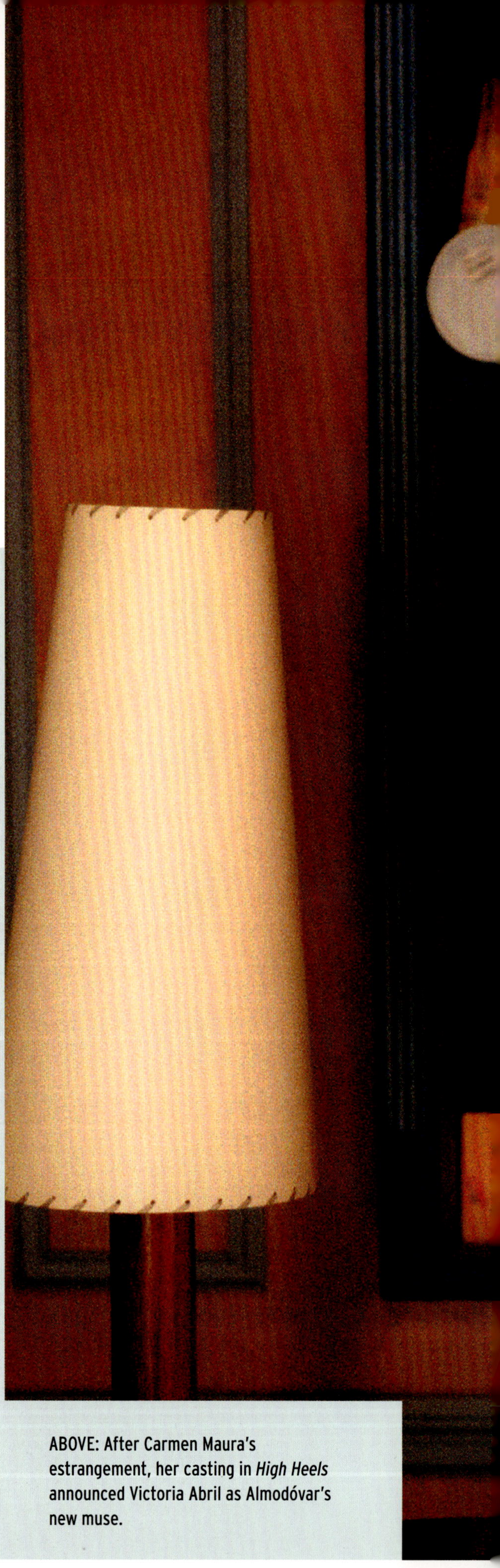

ABOVE: After Carmen Maura's estrangement, her casting in *High Heels* announced Victoria Abril as Almodóvar's new muse.

High Heels is Almodóvar's first great work about negligent motherhood, depicting how traumatic maternal separation from one's children can lead to reunion and redemption. Later films such as *Volver* or *All About My Mother* also explore the figure of the imperfect mother who manages to re-establish emotional ties – with her own family or with a new and unexpected one – to become, if only for an instant, the person she always should have been. Almodóvar's films are, above all, an ode to the strong and devoted mother, but also show empathy and compassion to those women who at some point have failed their children but find the integrity – and the love – to make amends.

The plot of *High Heels* includes a third character of some importance: Judge Domínguez, the investigating magistrate in charge of the case, whose split personality in different identities or 'disguises' allows him to go undercover to investigate possible suspects. His main alter ego, Femme Letal, a transvestite, is based on the style and look of Becky del Páramo. Antonio Banderas was to have played him, but the siren song of Hollywood led him to abandon the production just before it began and forced Almodóvar to postpone filming for six months to find a replacement. In a move not without risk, the director ended up choosing Miguel Bosé, son of the famous bullfighter Luis Miguel Dominguín, and one of the most successful singers in the country. Despite some debate about the choice, Bosé – who had been working in cinema since the mid-seventies with filmmakers such as Dario Argento and Fernando Colomo – knew how to give the character the enigmatic aura required and made Femme Letal one of the great Almodóvarian characters of the decade.

After the experience with Ennio Morricone in *Tie Me Up! Tie Me Down!*, Almodóvar turned for the score to the highly regarded Ryuichi Sakamoto, who had won an Oscar four years earlier for his work on *The Last Emperor* (Bernardo Bertolucci, 1987). However, Almodóvar ended up discarding most of the music created by Sakamoto, feeling that it did not fit the tone of the story, and did not correspond to his vision (years later, the composer would admit that he knew almost nothing about Spain and that Almodóvar did the right thing by removing his pieces). Instead, the director opted to include several songs from his personal miscellany, such as 'Soleá' and 'Saeta', by Miles Davis, 'C'est irreparable', by Nino Ferrer, and even a couple of compositions by George Fenton from *Dangerous Liaisons* (Stephen Frears, 1988). Despite this, it was the two songs interpreted expressly for the film by the Galician artist Luz Casal – the adaptation of 'Piensa en mí' by Agustín Lara and Chavela Vargas, and 'Un año de amor' by Gaby Verlor, with lyrics by the filmmaker himself – that turned the soundtrack into a bestseller and one of the musical highlights of Spanish cinema.

RIGHT ABOVE: The director rehearses with Miguel Bosé (Letal) for one of his extravagant musical performances.

RIGHT: Rebeca's live on-air murder confession was the first scene Almodóvar devised for the film.

“IT WASN'T EASY, BECAUSE I WANTED THE CHARACTER TO BE NEITHER A MONSTER NOR A PSYCHOPATH.”

LEFT: *High Heels* was Almodóvar's breakthrough in France, where he won the César Award for Best Foreign Film.

ALMODÓVAR'S FILMS ARE, ABOVE ALL, AN ODE TO THE STRONG AND DEVOTED MOTHER.

Exhibiting a sure-footed maturity, *High Heels* showcases Almodóvar's ability to combine with surprising naturalness two seemingly contrary genres: melodrama and crime thriller. The shadow of Douglas Sirk hovers over the whole story, especially his classic *Imitation of Life* (1959), which narrated the stormy relationship between a movie star and her daughter. Almodóvar drew direct inspiration from Lana Turner's character in the film for Marisa Paredes's hairstyle. However, it is not the only film referenced by the director, who also made use of the maternal-filial conflicts of titles such as *Stella Dallas* (King Vidor, 1937), *Mildred Pierce* (Michael Curtiz, 1945), *Terms of Endearment* (James L. Brooks, 1983) and *Postcards from the Edge* (Mike Nichols, 1990) to shape the story of Becky and Rebeca. From all of them he extracted a dramatic potential which is omnipresent in the film, sitting happily alongside other genres ranging from film noir to comedy, including the musical through the iconic prison choreography.

While the critical reception was ambivalent, commercially it was one of the greatest successes of Almodóvar's career to date, attracting an audience of nearly two million in Spain. It was a blockbuster in France too, where it also won the César Award for Best Foreign Film of the year. In Chile, the reaction was more extreme; three men, belonging to a 'moralistic league' and determined to stop the film from being seen, stole the only copy after a preview in a cinema in the capital. It had a modest commercial run in the United States but did receive a Golden Globe nomination, prompting actors of the calibre of Jodie Foster, Glenn Close and Susan Sarandon to publicly express their desire to work with the director. Publications as prestigious as *Liberation*, *The Guardian* and *Vanity Fair* dedicated extensive features to a radiant Almodóvar. The international recognition once again had its strange counterpoint in a lack of success at the Goya Awards, the film not winning in any of the five technical categories it was nominated. Unfathomably, neither the director nor his two leading actors (whose performances are among the best in his filmography) received a nomination.

KIKA

KIKA (1993)

'As always, I wrote it just for fun, to detox. Also, as always, at the beginning it was a translation of my needs. The world around me and my own world threatened to suffocate me, and I needed a good dose of optimism. I wanted to recover for my life and for my cinema the fresh breath of comedy.' When Pedro Almodóvar began to contemplate his next lead during the long promotional trips for *High Heels*, he found himself giving shape to a stunning character, a woman full of life, probably the most naive and charming of all his imagined characters. He saw her as an injection of positivity after the dramatic intensity of his most recent films, a perfect mix between Marilyn Monroe, the Audrey Hepburn of *Breakfast at Tiffany's* (Blake Edwards, 1961) and two of his own creations: the emblematic Patty Diphusa and Candela, played by María Barranco in *Women on the Verge of a Nervous Breakdown*. But, as the story progressed, much shadier characters began to break through until the film descended into an unexpected darkness, a spiral from which the director could not – nor wanted to – escape.

Almodóvar knew very well which actor he should cast for a character like Kika. In *What Have I Done to Deserve This?*, Verónica Forqué had already sketched a first outline of this make-up artist with an indelible smile: Cristal, the sex worker who was always positive no matter how hard life became. Almodóvar, though, links Cristal and Kika much more darkly; Cristal submits to men, sometimes violently, through her toil as a sex worker, while Kika has been the victim of rape by a porn actor; these are both women who suffer in a male world, where any ray of light can be easily extinguished.

In this way, a film that starts like a screwball comedy of contagious optimism (alongside Forqué, Rossy de Palma features once again, giving a hilarious performance as her assistant) is transformed into a dark and sinister thriller, loaded with fatalism and social commentary. *Kika* also features two of the most diabolical characters ever

ABOVE: In her third consecutive film with Almodóvar, Victoria Abril played the role of the unscrupulous television star Andrea.

> *KIKA* HAS REMARKABLE ASPECTS THAT I'M PROUD OF, BUT IT WAS IMPOSSIBLE TO JUDGE THEM IN SUCH A TENSE ATMOSPHERE.

LEFT: Despite being his most reviled film, Almodóvar has always been pleased with *Kika*'s risky and irreverent combination of genres.

created by its director: the writer and serial killer Nicholas Pierce (Peter Coyote), and the ferocious and resentful Andrea Caracortada (Victoria Abril), creator and presenter of an outrageously exploitative reality television show. Almodóvar took the idea from a series of programmes he had seen on American television, as at that time, this type of unscrupulous reality TV had not yet arrived in Spain. Sometime later, the arrival of these formats on most of the country's channels would confirm, once again, the filmmaker's prophetic nature and his ability to intuit social transformations.

Since its premiere, *Kika* has had the aura of a cursed work among Almodóvar's films, an exaggerated and unfair label – it is neither a bad film, nor the worst made by the director – but the result of a particular moment in the country's history. In 1992, Spain had become the epicentre of world news thanks to the Olympic Games being staged in Barcelona, the Universal Exhibition in Seville – which, coincidentally, premiered Almodóvar's unreleased short film *Salomé* – and the fifth centenary of the discovery of America. This sudden international focus on the country translated into a period of (fleeting) economic growth and sociocultural optimism. As a result, the cultural spotlight shone on Spanish creators of all kinds who were feted with unbridled enthusiasm; that year, Spanish cinema won only its second Oscar with *Belle Époque*. Directed by Fernando Trueba, that brilliant and restrained period drama is a clear reflection of the kind of image that the industry tried to export to the rest of the world.

When *Kika* hit screens in 1993, there were many who were appalled by, as they saw it, its celebration of evil as a destructive force, of corrupting a comedy starring a forceful woman and transforming it into a dark reflection of real life. Critics circled and Almodóvar attracted the anger of many feminists who, when details of the film's story were leaked, criticised the comic treatment of rape in the film, which thankfully led him to discard the crass *An Inopportune Rape* as one of the film's possible titles (other titles that were considered were *The Eyes of Tamil*, *A Horrible Summer Day*, *The Murderer's Nails* and a female version of *The Good, the Bad and the Ugly*). '*Kika* has remarkable aspects that I'm proud of, but it was impossible to judge them in such a tense atmosphere because of political correctness,' recalls the director. 'I think we are now more aware that humour cannot aspire to be politically correct, and that it can serve to deal with the most serious and painful aspects of life, including rape.' Among the cited references for the justification of the controversial scene were *Torn Curtain* (Alfred Hitchcock, 1966) and *Blood Simple* (Joel Coen, 1984).

The critical and commercial success of his films to date had positioned Almodóvar at the peak of Spanish cinema. Few directors enjoyed his international prestige, and his stories exuded the mark of a pure and indomitable author. It is possible that, for all this, his expectations for *Kika* were overly ambitious: a 700 million pesetas budget and fourteen weeks of shooting, both the highest figures of his career. It included an exclusive wardrobe for Victoria Abril's character designed by Jean Paul Gaultier and another for Verónica Forqué by Gianni Versace, and the inclusion, for the first time in one of his films, of a Hollywood actor (Peter Coyote, fresh from filming *Bitter Moon* with Roman Polanski). These extremely high expectations were soon dashed by the bad smell that seemed to follow the film wherever it went. It received terrible reviews and a smear campaign that even spread abroad, where adverts for the film featuring Victoria Abril's fake breasts were banned on London's buses and in the pages of *The New York Times*, supposedly 'to avoid giving offence.'

Kika was a failure, not because of its disappointing – although by no means catastrophic – box office, the scant harvest of awards (despite everything, Forqué won a well-deserved Goya for Best Actress) or the disaffection it caused among Almodóvar's enthusiasts. What hurt the film, and its author, was the fierce campaign that, paradoxically, accused him of taking risks and entering uncomfortable terrain from a formal and narrative point of view. 'It's the closest my career has ever come to going bankrupt,' he admitted. 'There was an extraordinarily negative unanimity towards *Kika*. That's why I used the word lynching. I don't want to fall into the easy resource of talking about envy or settling scores, nor do I want to feel like a victim. I prefer to analyse everything calmly. Fortunately, the film has tremendous strength and will end up surviving, like Kika herself.'

RIGHT: The fabulous work of Verónica Forqué (Kika) and Rossy de Palma (Juana) creates the film's most hilarious moments.

THE FLOWER OF MY SECRET

THE FLOWER OF MY SECRET

La flor de mi secreto (1995)

For Pedro Almodóvar, *The Flower of My Secret* was an exercise in reconciliation on all levels after the furore generated by *Kika*: with the public and critics, and of course, with the classic melodrama of his previous films. But, above all, his eleventh film represented a return to the major themes such as life at the crossroads and heartbreak, the suffering of female characters and the vindication of the mother as the driving force of the family. A story without villains – 'like Frank Capra's' – where pain is shown but also tenacity and hope, and in which Almodóvar pays tribute to his first love, storytelling.

'I wanted to be a writer from my earliest childhood, and when I was only eight years old, I was already writing my own fiction stories,' he recalls. 'My aspiration was to write a great novel, although, as time went by, reality showed me that what I wrote ended up becoming little films. I understood that those texts were not literary stories, but sketches of film scripts.' Little by little, Almodóvar knew that he had to express his inner world through the lens of a camera and not on the pages of a book: 'On more than one occasion I have been asked to write my autobiography and I have always refused; I have also been asked to have someone else write it, but I still feel a kind of allergy to seeing a book that talks entirely about me as a person.' By directly invoking such an intrinsic part of his personality, *The Flower of My Secret* can be seen as a very intimate process of affirmation (and healing) by a director who, for the first time in his very successful career, had looked into the abyss of failure.

As in *High Heels*, the genesis of *The Flower of My Secret* lies in a specific situation imagined by Almodóvar, and his deep desire to

RIGHT: Marisa Paredes is stunning in her role as a woman, Leo, in complete emotional breakdown.

“I WANTED TO BE A WRITER FROM MY EARLIEST CHILDHOOD.”

see it projected on a screen. The scene involved a lonely woman who receives an unexpected visit from her husband, a high-ranking military officer deployed to Bosnia, and ends up being abandoned soon after. She refuses to accept that the love between them has ended and tries to win him back with a desperate question, which the filmmaker would eventually turn into the provisional title of his project: *Is there any possibility, however small, of saving what is ours?* Almodóvar began to develop the before and after of that moment, a process that entailed many revisions leading to eight different versions of the script, one of the most laborious writing processes of his career. The final script would feature a romance writer named Leo Macías, who, in the middle of a creative block due to the breakup with her husband, decides she needs to write a noir genre work. Marisa Paredes took the role of Leo (although Ana Belén was originally considered for the role), alongside Carme Elías as Betty, Leo's best friend, Juan Echanove as Ángel, an editor at *El País*, and Imanol Arias, who returned to the director's universe thirteen years after *Labyrinth of Passion*, as the absent husband.

In Almodóvar's films, colour evokes situations and emotions, portraying the inner journey of the main character, and has, without exception, a specific dramatic meaning. In *The Flower of My Secret*, it is used as a fundamental element to explore the confusing and changing personality of the protagonist, someone who dedicates herself to writing romantic, pink, novels under a pseudonym that refers, precisely, to an absence of colour: Amanda Gris (Amanda Grey). 'If a writer like Leo, out of absent-mindedness or pain, contemplates herself in the black mirror of reality, she will cross the border that divides two genres as opposite and neighbouring as Pink and Black,' explained the filmmaker. To further emphasise his point he borrowed one of his favourite phrases from *Casablanca* (Michael Curtiz, 1942) for the moment when Ángel (Juan Echanove) shares his feelings for Leo in the Plaza Mayor in Madrid, reminding her that she was wearing blue the day they met. 'Bogart was telling Ingrid Bergman that he remembered the day he saw her for the first

LEFT: After anticipating a loving reunion with her husband Paco (Imanol Arias), Leo is instead devastated when he ends their relationship.

RIGHT: Almodóvar and Marisa Paredes rehearse the moment of Leo's passionate confrontation with Paco.

time, during the occupation of Paris, because the Germans were wearing grey, and she was wearing blue. It is impossible to express more emotion. . . And all that Bogart did was make a comment about clothes.'

The paths of Almodóvar and Leo run parallel; they are both artists who tell stories, have suffered a setback and are looking to rediscover their identity. While in pre-production, the director received a call from his sister telling him that his mother had asked to see a psychiatrist so she could talk to someone. Realising that his widowed mother must be intensely lonely, he planned a trip to see her and record their conversations on film. However, he was unable to take the trip, but he did plan one for Leo, who, in her moment of greatest despair, decides to seek solace with her mother (Chus Lampreave), who is eager to leave the city and return to her village home. 'From the beginning, Chus has officially represented my mother, because she knows it and because the three or four characters inspired by my mother have been made by her,' Almodóvar would admit years later. 'Of course, in *The Flower of My Secret*, absolutely all of the phrases that she says were said by my mother.'

It was in this way, with a return to one's roots through the mother, that Almodóvar and Leo find a way to recover their motivation and instinct. The scenes that take place in Almagro – located thirty kilometres from Calzada de Calatrava, Almodóvar's hometown in Ciudad Real – are like a breath of fresh air after the suffocation of the city and are wrapped in a distinct halo of poetry and simplicity. 'I photographed the fields of red earth, infinite, glued directly to the sky,' he said.

Lampreave hadn't worked with Almodóvar since *Women on the Verge of a Nervous Breakdown*, but she delivered one of the most famous and repeated lines of his films: *Cara de ladilla* (Crab face); a Spanish expletive that her character calls her youngest daughter every time she gets annoyed and fed up with her.

“I PHOTOGRAPHED THE FIELDS OF RED EARTH, INFINITE, GLUED DIRECTLY TO THE SKY.”

MOTHER: **Oh, my daughter, what a pity. . . Your father must be turning in his grave!**

ROSA: **(Trying to take the phone away from her) Leo!**

MOTHER: **Shut up, crab face! Listen, I'm going back to the village and my house where I can get some peace.**

LEO: **I'm going with you. I'll pick you up right away and take you in the car.**

MOTHER: **You're coming with me? Oh, I'm so happy!**

ROSA: **Leo, don't listen to her! Nobody here has thrown her out of the house!**

MOTHER: **No? Your husband!**

ROSA: **My husband? Leo, Santiago didn't throw her out, all he told her is that no one must give him permission to drink in his house! What were you thinking, calling him a drunkard to his face?**

MOTHER: **Because he is!**

ROSA: **You don't know anything!**

MOTHER: **You're the one who doesn't know anything! What do you want me to do, stand here with my mouth shut? You treat me like a dog!**

The Flower of My Secret was the first collaboration between Almodóvar and the musician Alberto Iglesias, born in San Sebastián in 1955, a professional relationship that has been maintained ever since and has given rise to some of the best scores of his career. At that time, Iglesias was one of the most promising composers in Spanish cinema, thanks mainly to his work with Julio Medem in *Cows* (*Vacas*, 1991) and *The Red Squirrel* (*La ardilla roja*, 1993), two films in which he demonstrated his great ability to transmit very deep emotions using few resources, some as unusual as the *txalaparta*, a traditional Basque percussion instrument. Captivated by the composer's artistic personality, Almodóvar set him the challenge of creating music that would represent the intense pain that afflicts Leo, something that Iglesias achieved thanks to his impressive mastery of string instruments, in this case the viola, violin and cello. Despite this, the director – still bruised and wary from the disappointing experiences with Morricone and Sakamoto – decided to include only part of Iglesias's work in the film, completing the soundtrack with songs by Caetano Veloso, Bola de Nieve, and Chavela Vargas. But learning from his experience, Alberto Iglesias adapted to the style and requirements of Almodóvar, and the two have developed a very fruitful creative relationship.

Through the film, Almodóvar returned to his central theme of female redemption, depicting women who live subjugated to the archetype of the Iberian *macho*: selfish, unfaithful and dominant men who no longer love them. As part of their journey, they will lose their way, and may even mourn their loneliness, but they will receive the support of family, and discover that, far from those toxic male figures, they can be themselves, raise their voices, and live and love freely. For these reasons, *The Flower of My Secret* occupies a central position in Almodóvar's cinema, a title of enormous artistic depth where previous stories and the ideal of the feminine universe come to converge in glorious fullness.

ABOVE: Chus Lampreave (Leo's mother) and Rossy de Palma (Rosa) once again deliver superb comedy performances.

FAR LEFT: Leo is consumed by heartbreak.

LEFT: The director, ready to start shooting.

FAMILI

LIVE FLESH

LIVE FLESH

Carne trémula (1997)

Once Almodóvar regained his artistic pulse thanks to *The Flower of My Secret*, he began work on what would be his strangest and seemingly most alien film to date. *Live Flesh*, besides being his first pure noir without concessions to melodrama or comedy, is considered a rarity in Almodóvar's career for several reasons, most notably because it is the first feature film adapted from foreign material – in this case, a 1986 novel by the British mystery writer Ruth Rendell – and the first for which he shared screenplay credit. In an unusual six-handed exercise, that he would never repeat, Almodóvar turned to two young Spanish writing talents for his adaptation: the cult novelist Ray Loriga and the Asturian screenwriter Jorge Guerricaechevarría, the latter responsible for the script of one of the great successes of Spanish cinema of the nineties, *The Day of the Beast* (*El día de la bestia*, Álex de la Iglesia, 1995).

The approach to the story also presented two substantial variations. The first of these occurs in the prologue, set in 1970, during which a young woman gives birth on a bus while the Franco regime decrees the State of Exception, a crackdown on political protest and student revolts. This is the first explicit reference to the dictatorship that we find in a film by Almodóvar, who until then had always argued that the best revenge against Franco was to ignore him completely, as if he had never existed. After the opening sequence, the plot moves forward two decades and depicts the unhappy life of Víctor, the bus baby turned pizza delivery boy who is sent to prison for beating up a policeman named David, who was trying to intervene in a fight between Víctor and Elena, a young drug addict. During the confrontation, Víctor shoots David leaving him partially but severely paralysed. After he has served his sentence, Víctor tries to reconcile with Elena, but she is now married to David, now a famous wheelchair basketball player for the Spanish Olympic team, who tells

RIGHT: Victor (Liberto Rabal) threatens Elena (Francesca Neri) during the explosive beginning of the film.

LIVE FLESH IS AN ANOMALY WITHIN ALMODÓVAR'S BODY OF WORK.

LEFT: True to his exhaustive preparation, Javier Bardem learned to play wheelchair basketball with amazing skill.

Víctor to keep away. In this way, *Live Flesh* is an anomaly within Almodóvar's body of work to date, since it is the first – though later films *Bad Education*, *The Skin I Live In* and *Pain and Glory* would follow suit – in which the male characters carry the weight of the story almost exclusively. Almodóvar's male characters tend to be erratic and immature, in stark contrast to the integrity and strength of his women: 'As a dramatic subject, I am much more interested in men when they start to be men, like Víctor. I don't see myself writing stories about forty-somethings who have problems with their love lives.'

As well as changing his working methods, the director dispensed with his usual stable of returning performers, thinking that perhaps they were too attached to a style from which *Live Flesh* was intentionally trying to escape. Of the main characters, only Javier Bardem (David), who had a very brief role in *High Heels*, had worked with the director before, with Jorge Sanz – then one of the most glittering stars in the Spanish industry – in the role of Víctor. The cast was rounded out with the Italian Francesca Neri (well known in Spain for her work with Bigas Luna in *The Ages of Lulu* and Carlos Saura in *Outrage*) as Elena, and the acclaimed José Sancho and Ángela Molina playing a married couple, Sancho and Clara, mired in obsession and jealousy. Almodóvar put his cast through four months of intense rehearsals, time that Bardem took advantage of to learn how to play wheelchair basketball with amazing skill.

Shooting began in early January 1997 – days before, the Christmas-decorated Arenal Street in Madrid was used for one scene – but soon disagreements arose between Almodóvar and Jorge Sanz, who openly challenged the director's methods in front of the rest of the crew. After a week of filming, both agreed that the best thing was to start again with a new actor: Sanz exited by mutual consent, receiving his full salary of ten million pesetas, and El Deseo began a frantic search for a replacement. On 1 February, Liberto Rabal, grandson of the legendary Paco Rabal (who had played a film director in *Tie Me Up! Tie Me Down!*), and a promising newcomer who had just starred in his first film, *Tramway to Malvarrosa* (*Tranvía a la Malvarrosa*, José Luis García Sánchez, 1997), for which he was nominated for a Goya as Best New Actor, was added to the cast. However, this was not to be Almodóvar's only headache, as he had to deal with one of the hottest and least rainy winters in Spain in living memory: 'For the location shooting, I had hoped to have those overcast skies, full of dark clouds like smoke, which are so typical of Madrid. But nature was not on my side, so instead of grey skies, we suffered insistently from blazing sun. I had no choice but to accept it as an imposition of fate.'

Fate, however, would also place before him the most important performer of his later career. When she first received Almodóvar's call, Penélope Cruz was twenty-two years old and was already regarded as one of the greatest actors in Spain. In *Live Flesh*, her role was limited to the prologue, in which she would play the young woman giving birth to her child on a lonely bus. 'As soon as we got to the set, Pedro and I would go into a room to practise animal moans, because he said that I was very fine and that I couldn't be that fine in the film,' recalled the Madrid-born actor. Despite the brevity of the role, Cruz began to establish herself as the quintessential representation of motherhood in the director's work – it was no accident that Almodóvar named her character Isabel Plaza Caballero, in clear reference

ABOVE: Francesca Neri enjoyed considerable popularity in Spain thanks to her previous work with Carlos Saura.

RIGHT: Victor, a character in constant search of redemption.

FAR RIGHT: The prologue, set in 1970, was the only reference to Francoism.

26 DIEGO DE LEON
M-975578
SP

RIGHT: ***Live Flesh*** **marked Penélope Cruz's debut in Almodóvar's universe. From the outset, her character was facing a difficult motherhood.**

to his mother's surname – lauded over time for her extraordinary performances in *Volver*, *Pain and Glory* and *Parallel Mothers*.

Despite being unusual within the director's canon, *Live Flesh* is full of many familiar Almodóvarian themes: violence, resilience, redemption and obsessive love. That he was able to take another author's work, in another genre, and adapt it so successfully to his style demonstrated a previously untapped side of the director. He described it as 'an intense drama, baroque and sensual, totally independent of the Ruth Rendell novel that inspired it, which resides in the classic thriller and tragedy.' However, the film – which was seen by an audience of 1.4 million and was nominated for a BAFTA for Best Foreign Film – suffers at times from the inconsistency shown by Almodóvar throughout the decade, alternating passages of excellent cinematography and narrative pulse with others that are much more dispensable, mainly, in retrospect, due to some questionable casting decisions. Today, *Live Flesh* can be regarded as a *rara avis*, as curious as it is attractive, and as a precursor to the explosion that was about to take place.

> “I WOULD GO INTO A ROOM TO PRACTISE ANIMAL MOANS, BECAUSE HE SAID THAT I WAS VERY FINE AND THAT I COULDN'T BE THAT FINE IN THE FILM.”
>
> PENÉLOPE CRUZ

ALL ABOUT MY MOTHER

ALL ABOUT MY MOTHER

Todo sobre mi madre (1999)

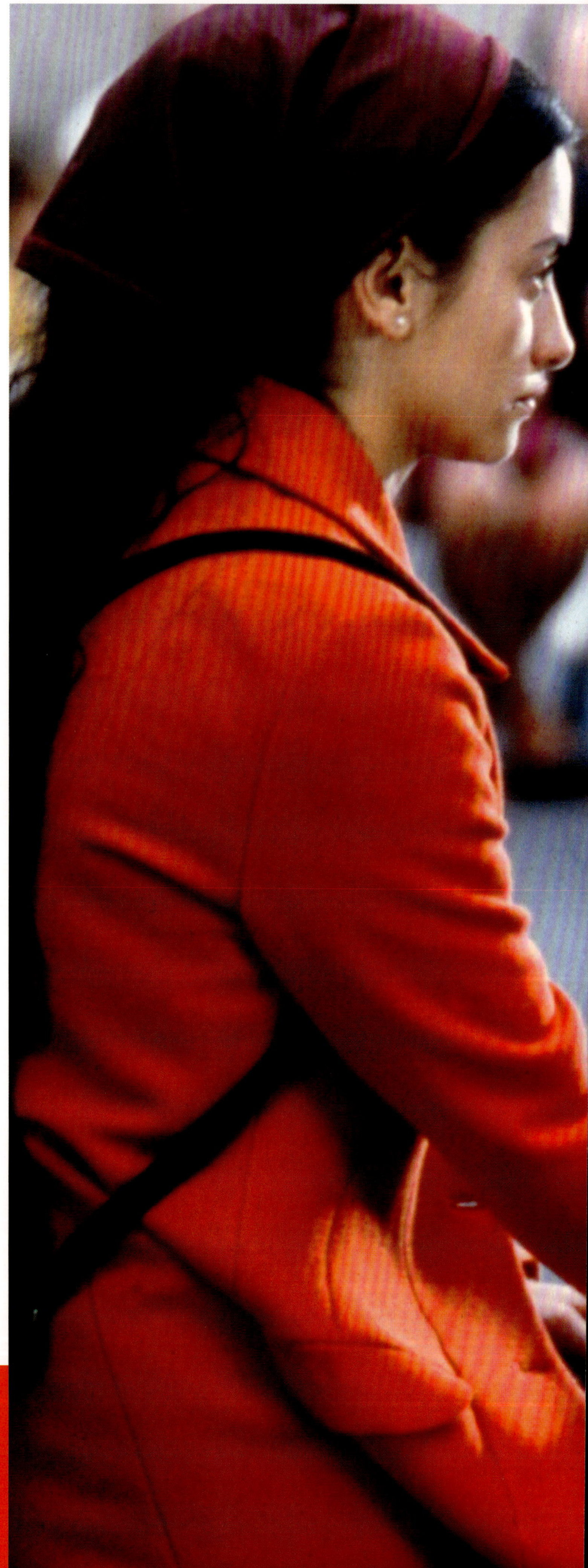

All About My Mother is a film born of enthusiasm. From the first stirrings of the story, Almodóvar was overtaken with a contagious passion for the magnitude of the project. 'I think it will be my most moving film,' he said shortly before production began.

The initial concept arose from the opening scenes of *The Flower of My Secret*, in which a nurse played by Kiti Mánver role-plays a mother's grief over the death of her son during a seminar on organ transplants. 'I had the idea of making a film about the acting ability of certain people who are not actors,' he explained, once again fascinated by the kaleidoscopic effect of watching someone play a role within a role. After drawing inspiration, once again, from his vast cinephile knowledge – Gena Rowlands in *Opening Night* (John Cassavetes, 1977) and Romy Schneider in *That Most Important Thing: Love* (*L'important c'est d'aimer*, Andrzej Żulawski, 1975) were cited references – Almodóvar developed 'a story of women with great conflicts,' two characters connected by the figure of Blanche DuBois, the maddened and tragic protagonist of Tennessee Williams's *A Streetcar Named Desire*.

Like the fleeting character in *The Flower of My Secret*, Manuela (Cecilia Roth) is a nurse who supervises donor organ transplants in a hospital in Madrid and who, at times, tries her luck as an amateur actor. Her teenage son Esteban (Eloy Azorín) longs to know more about his absent father, whose identity Manuela has never revealed. On the night of his seventeenth birthday, just as his mother has decided to tell him the whole truth, Esteban is run over and killed

RIGHT: Fifteen years after her last appearance in an Almodóvar film, Cecilia Roth (Manuela) is the driving force in this captivating story about loss and solidarity among women.

> **THIS UNUSUAL MODEL OF THE ALMODÓVARIAN MOTHER FIGURE WILL END UP BROKEN BY TRAGEDY.**

while trying to get an autograph from stage actor Huma Rojo (Marisa Paredes), who is starring in an adaptation of *A Streetcar Named Desire*. In unbelievable pain, Manuela travels to Barcelona to fulfil her last promise and find Esteban's father, a transvestite named Lola.

Despite the apparent evidence of its title, *All About My Mother* is not an autobiographical film, nor does it offer the usual Francisca Caballero-inspired depiction of motherhood. In fact, it was named in homage to another of the director's favourite films, *All About Eve* (Joseph L. Mankiewicz, 1950), in which an ageing diva, Bette Davis, is transmuted into another fictional one, Margo Channing, through an extraordinary exercise in narrative symbiosis. The Manuela of *All About My Mother* is an independent and modern woman, someone who does not need to be subjected to the macho whims and behaviour of a man and chooses to raise her son alone. However, this unusual model of the Almodóvarian mother figure will end up broken by tragedy, giving rise to one of the most brilliant portrayals of pain and loss in contemporary cinema. Almodóvar had never given himself to melodrama with such intensity, causing terrible suffering to run amok through his female lead's life. But he had also never shown such hope in the face of tragedy, strength drawn from the joyful support of wounded sisters (not by chance – one of the titles considered by the director was *The Kindness of Strangers*). In doing so, Almodóvar presents the audience with a new example of a family model composed of kind and compassionate individuals, who share their sorrows in order to fight adversity together.

All About My Mother reimagines Almodóvar's traditional view that only the power and love of the mother can redeem past wrongs (*High Heels*) or resolve traumas (*The Flower of My Secret*), instead showing that the mother can feel unresolved pain, not least when searching for a missing son. Approaching fifty, Almodóvar changed his point of view and moved in the opposite direction, showing the older character suffering in a way that previously only affected the children. 'Everyone wants to be a mother,' acknowledged the filmmaker, who assumed a point of view that would recur in his later work. 'It doesn't matter the sex because there are many ways to express motherhood, we all want to conceive, and Manuela won't stop until she finds a way to replace that dead son.' Manuela's

ABOVE: The director and his leading actress pose in front of the emblematic entrance of the theatre where *A Streetcar Named Desire* is performed.

new, makeshift family includes Rosa (Penélope Cruz, pregnant again to illustrate the perfect image of motherhood), a giggly, HIV-infected nun, and Agrado (Antonia San Juan), a transsexual sex worker who brings a gallows humour to the darkest corners of life. Most memorable is the sequence in which Agrado delivers an improvised monologue about her life, which was inspired by the true story of the Argentinian actor Lola Membrives, who, after an electrical failure at the theatre she was performing in, told a story to the audience about her own experiences until the power returned.

I THINK THE SUCCESS LIES PRECISELY IN THE FACT THAT, DESPITE THE WILDNESS OF THE STORY, THE PEOPLE WHO SEE THE FILM FEEL VERY CLOSE TO ITS PROFOUND IDEAS.

LEFT: The partnership between Almodóvar and Penélope Cruz, who plays the radiant Rosa, was already formidable.

AGRADO: My friend and I want to get off the street, but we have to work, don't we, Manolita? Whatever, even if it's cleaning stairs. We don't care.

ROSA: The truth is that there's not much else... Well, garbage collectors... Or learning how to make crafts here in the workshop, petit-point tablecloths, centrepieces of dried flowers...

AGRADO: Well, I'd almost prefer to be a garbage collector.

ROSA: And what do you know how to do, apart from the street?

MANUELA: I've worked as a cook in a restaurant.

AGRADO: She's half a surgeon. Look at my face... She did it to me [...] She's related to Lola.

ROSA: Oh yeah? And do you know what's happened to her?

MANUELA: I haven't seen her for more than eighteen years.

AGRADO: She robbed my house.

ROSA: Well, she was here, about four months ago. We helped her detox [...] If you see her, tell her I'd like to say goodbye before going to El Salvador.

AGRADO: You're going to El Salvador? Maybe I'll come too... I've always thought I could do well in the developing world [...] Here, the street is getting worse every day, sister. Even if we had little competition from the whores, the drags are sweeping us away. I can't stand the drags. They're a bunch of mamarrachas [...]

ROSA: In El Salvador I don't think there's much drag, but they're in full guerrilla mode.

AGRADO: Oh yeah? I didn't know that.

ROSA: I'm going to replace some nuns who were murdered.

AGRADO: Well, I don't know if the best thing for me right now is a guerrilla.

MANUELA: Oh, you're such a brute, Agrado.

RIGHT: The filmmaker with two of his most treasured collaborators, Cecilia Roth and Marisa Paredes, reunited for the first time since *Dark Habits*.

Cecilia Roth's powerful portrayal of Manuela is the soul of *All About My Mother*, or, as Almodóvar put it, 'the marrow, because she is the woman I follow with the camera and who takes us through the different stories of the film.' A cast regular in his early films, Roth had been absent from his universe for fifteen years; in that time, she had become one of the most respected Latin American actors worldwide, with acclaimed appearances in *A Place in the World* (*Un lugar en el mundo*, 1992) and *Martín (Hache)* (1997), both directed by Adolfo Aristarain. 'I don't know how, during the three months that the shooting lasted, she knew how to contain herself and be beyond pain, but always reflecting it,' Almodóvar commented on a role that earned Roth a dozen international awards. 'I loved Manuela a lot,' she recalled. 'Like me, she came from a faraway country, wanted to invent a life in another place and managed, putting one brick on top of another, to put together that life more or less similar to the one of her dreams.'

Undoubtedly, one of the most moving and powerful passages of the film is when we hear Manuela's voice-over, on board a train to Barcelona, explaining the reason for that journey to redemption. Accompanied by the chords of the song 'Tajabone', by the Senegalese musician Ismaël Lô, the city appears in all its grandeur before the viewer's eyes. After almost two decades of stories set in Madrid, Almodóvar found in Barcelona the ideal place to locate Manuela's emotional journey; somehow, the Mediterranean spirit and the modernist architecture of the city provided a balm to the suffering of his characters. Approximately eighty per cent of the scenes take place there, with locations as picturesque and representative as the Sagrada Familia, the Borne, the Gothic Quarter, the Plaza Real and the seaside district of La Barceloneta.

Surprisingly, a film directed by Pedro Almodóvar achieved both unanimous critical and public acclaim for the first time. *All About My Mother* became a resounding triumph practically from the moment of its release, reaching an audience of 2.5 million in Spain alone – where it played in theatres for sixty weeks – and winning a total of seven Goya Awards, including Best Film, Director and Lead Actress. Its international success was even more extraordinary, with a global gross of $68 million and more than fifty awards, including the award for Best Foreign Language Film at the Golden Globe, BAFTA, César and David di Donatello awards, plus the award for Best Director at the Cannes Film Festival. In the words of its author, 'I think the success lies precisely in the fact that, despite the wildness of the story, the people who see the film feel very close to its profound ideas.' The maelstrom of recognition reached its climax on 26 March 2000, at the Shrine Auditorium in Los Angeles, where Almodóvar picked up the Oscar for Best Foreign Language Film from Antonio Banderas and Penélope Cruz. That initial enthusiasm he felt while imagining the story had led to an undisputed masterpiece, a profoundly beautiful and inspiring artistic exaltation. The provocative and brazen young man from *La Movida* had become a revered filmmaker who, from that moment on, had earned his place in the history of cinema.

"EVERYONE WANTS TO BE A MOTHER...
WE ALL WANT TO CONCEIVE."

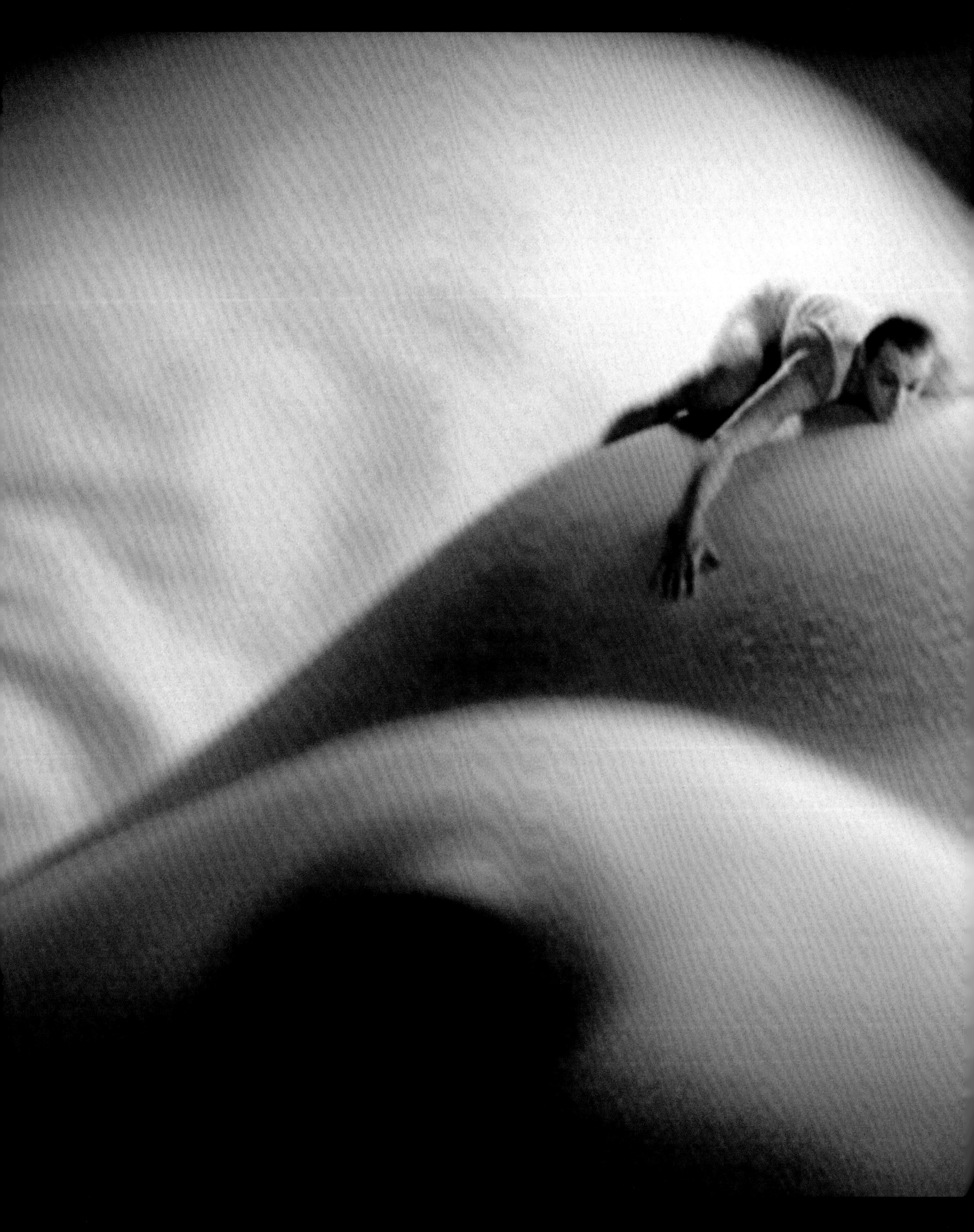

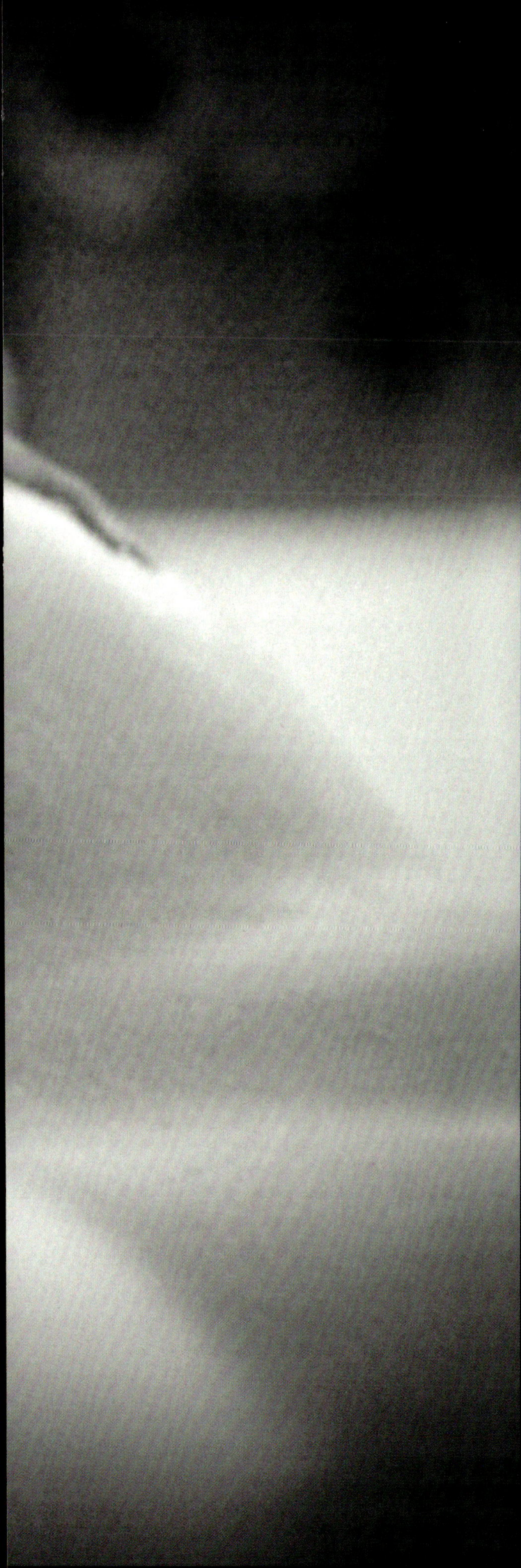

TALK TO HER

TALK TO HER

Hable con ella (2002)

In 1989, during his first promotional visit to Los Angeles for the Oscar nomination for *Women on the Verge of a Nervous Breakdown*, Almodóvar had the opportunity to meet one of his great idols, Billy Wilder. During the meal they shared, the legendary filmmaker gave him a piece of advice that has never left him: 'Never come to Hollywood. It doesn't matter what they can offer you.' Throughout the following decade, Almodóvar had little trouble dodging the proposals that came to him from American cinema, mainly because their artistic value (the musical comedy *Sister Act*, for example) was dubious to say the least. However, after winning the Oscar for *All About My Mother*, the quality of the offers increased considerably, making it more difficult for the director to deny the Hollywood temptation. Even so, he decided to return to Spain with the firm conviction of maintaining his creative independence and continuing to bet on his scripts, born from his own perception and inexhaustible sharpness.

While he was still in the United States, Almodóvar began to develop his next project, based on a series of real incidents that captured his attention. The first was the story of an American woman who woke up after sixteen years in a coma that, according to doctors, was irreversible. The second was the return to life of a young Romanian woman who had been presumed dead after the morgue guard abused her supposed corpse. And the third was the mysterious pregnancy of a New York girl who had been in a coma for nine years, and who had been raped by a clinical assistant. 'Human acts have many readings, and these

> NEVER COME TO HOLLYWOOD. IT DOESN'T MATTER WHAT THEY CAN OFFER YOU.
>
> BILLY WILDER

can be seen as a crime or as saving a life. I wanted to defend that dilemma,' said the director, for whom *Talk to Her* is, above all, 'a story about communication and non-communication, about the friendship between two men and the long convalescence caused by the wounds of passion. But also, about cinema as a subject of conversation, and about how a monologue in front of a person in silence can be an effective form of dialogue.'

Talk to Her is, in effect, the story of two lonely individuals whose destinies are intertwined by tragedy. Almodóvar wrote the character of Benigno, a nurse at a private clinic who lives hidden from others, with his friend Roberto Benigni in mind – hence the name – but he was unable to take on the role, leading the director to cast Javier Cámara, an immense and versatile actor who until then had only been cast in comic roles in film and television. Quite the opposite of Darío Grandinetti, a sober and prestigious Argentinian performer, who had worked with directors such as Juan Carlos Desanzo and Eliseo Subiela. Almodóvar cast him in the role of Marco, a writer who is in the same clinic as Benigno, watching over his beloved, Lydia (Rosario Flores), a bullfighter who remains in a state of unconsciousness after a serious injury. Meanwhile, Benigno is devoted to Alicia (Leonor Watling), a dancer who is also in a coma after a car accident. He shares with her a passion for literature and cinema, trapped by a love that cannot be reciprocated, but which he dreams of manifesting when she wakes up.

BENIGNO: **On my days off I started going to the ballet. I also go to the Film Archive. I watch all the silent films I can: German, American, Italian. . . Everything. Then I tell her everything I've seen. These last four years have been the richest of my life, taking care of Alicia, and doing the things she liked to do. Except travelling, of course.**

MARCO: **The opposite happens to me with Lydia [. . .] I can't even touch her. I don't recognise her body. I'm even incapable of helping the nurses turn her over in bed. And I feel very mean.**

BENIGNO: **Talk to her. Tell her.**

MARCO: **Yes, I'd like to, but she can't hear me.**

BENIGNO: **And how are you so sure they can't hear us?**

MARCO: **Because her brain is dead, Benigno.**

BENIGNO: **A woman's brain is a mystery. And in this state, even more so. You must take women into account, talk to them. To share a detail from time to time, to caress them suddenly. Remember that they exist, that they are alive, and that they matter to us. That's the only therapy, I can tell you from experience.**

MARCO: **And what experience do you have with women?**

BENIGNO: **Me? All of it. I've lived day and night with one for twenty years and I've been with Alicia for four years.**

As in *Kika*, the characters' futures will be changed by a rape. However, in this case, Almodóvar does not show the assault, but turns it, with all the terrible consequences that doing so entails, into a subtle demonstration of love. To illustrate this, he chooses a wonderful seven-minute piece entitled *El amante menguante* (*The Shrinking Lover*), in homage to the classic *The Incredible Shrinking Man* (Jack Arnold, 1957). This is a fake silent film that Benigno tells Alicia about on the night he decides to act on his desire for her, and in which a man (Fele

PREVIOUS PAGE: After tackling female fraternity in his previous film, Almodóvar explored the complicity between two men in love with women in comas.

ABOVE: The director observes, with an amused gesture, a conversation between Leonor Watling (Alicia) and Javier Cámara (Benigno).

RIGHT: Lydia (Rosario Flores) prepares for the bullfight in which she will be seriously injured.

Martínez) shrinks after ingesting a potion and decides to give himself to the woman he loves (Paz Vega) in the only way physically possible: by entering her through her vagina and staying inside her forever. Through this passage inserted in the middle of the story, Almodóvar conveys the consummation of something dreadful from the beauty of images that show an impossible love, emphasizing the profoundly poetic personality of a film where everything, even the most atrocious event, is sublimated to the power of ingenuity.

After the rape, Alicia becomes pregnant and Benigno is imprisoned, unaware that she regains consciousness after childbirth. That manifestation of his feelings, the rape, although unforgivable, brings Alicia back to life and allows her to resume her career as a dancer. That is the great paradox of *Talk to Her*: that the most unhealthy and cruel love can make death – or something terribly similar – become life. The story is incredibly moving and Almodóvar triumphantly tackles the extraordinarily complex challenge. This is partly due to the delicacy and sobriety he exhibits when dealing with such an uncompromising subject, and because of his ability to stir the viewer's emotions – and also those of some characters who cry without blushing – from the most genuine artistic expressions.

Almodóvar started shooting at the Théâtre de la Ville in Paris in June 2001, with Javier Aguirresarobe, one of European cinema's most highly regarded cinematographers, behind the camera. For the choreographed scenes that top and tail the film, Almodóvar sought out the German choreographer Pina Bausch, whose piece *Café Müller* he was convinced was 'specially designed for *Talk to Her*.' By chance, her troupe was performing another of her pieces, *Masurca Fogo*, in Paris at the same time, so he took a unit to record a dance from it that would feature at the film's end. The production of *Talk to Her* continued for over three months in various locations, including the bullrings of Aranjuez (Madrid) and Brihuega (Guadalajara), and the Cordoba town of Lucena, which received the film crew during the shock of the September 11 terrorist attacks. Almodóvar also used his own house, located thirty kilometres from Madrid, to film the scenes in which the Brazilian musician Caetano Veloso performs his interpretation of Tomás Méndez's classic 'Cucurrucucú Paloma', and in which friends such as Marisa Paredes, Cecilia Roth and Manuel Bandera appear as extras.

Talk to Her premiered in March 2002 amidst unprecedented attention, the result of the high expectations generated by the worldwide triumph of *All About My Mother*. 'I only consider being a genius, not merely great or wonderful. I can only move on a thin line called perfection,' said Almodóvar, as he gladly accepted the pressure. In Spain, the press applauded it as one of the best films of the year and moviegoers filled the theatres, although the real recognition would come again from abroad, with more than $64 million in global box

“COMBINES SENSUALITY, SPIRITUALITY AND PURE NARRATIVE JOY IN WONDERFULLY HARMONIOUS PROPORTIONS.

TIME OUT”

ABOVE: Leonor Watling practised yoga to keep her body in a state of maximum relaxation, controlling her breathing and keeping her body inert.

office and enthusiastic reviews from *Time Out* ('combines sensuality, spirituality and pure narrative joy in wonderfully harmonious proportions'), *USA Today* ('warmly humanistic and boldly innovative') and *The New York Times* ('you can't get it out of your heart'). Particularly striking was the snub once again from the Spanish Academy of Cinema, which decided to award a single Goya for Best Original Soundtrack and to nominate Fernando León de Aranoa's *Mondays in the Sun* (*Los lunes al sol*) as the candidate for the Oscar for the Best Foreign Language Film. In a formidable example of poetic justice, *Talk to Her* received two Oscar nominations for Best Director and Original Screenplay – both for Almodóvar – winning in the latter category ahead of Todd Haynes (*Far from Heaven*), Steven Zaillian (*Gangs of New York*) and Alfonso Cuarón (*Y tu mamá también*).

BAD EDUCATION

BAD EDUCATION

La mala educación (2004)

On occasions, Pedro Almodóvar has said that the script for *Bad Education* is the best he has ever written, and the one that took him the longest time to complete. At first it was a short story, 'full of adolescent fury' and written in the seventies from his own experiences as a child, when a student at the high school in Cáceres with Salesian and Franciscan fathers. In it, a transvestite returns to the school where he studied to blackmail the priests who assaulted him in his childhood: 'There was a lot of abuse, especially among the youngest children. I was ten years old. In the bedroom, at night, we would tell each other about our experiences. The rumours spread beyond the school walls, and, because there were so many cases, the school administration had to intervene. In the end, those responsible were sent, without punishment, to teach at a boarding school for adolescents.' Almodóvar took up the idea again in the 1990s, changing the vengeful tone of the initial draft in order to find a larger story that justified the whole tale. By then, the project had already become a feature film and was provisionally titled *La visita* (*The Visit*).

He planned to shoot the film right after *All About My Mother*, but, unable to find an actor for the lead who was equally attractive as a man and as a woman – Leonardo Sbaraglia and Eduardo Noriega were some of the names that paraded unsuccessfully through the casting – he decided to park it and concentrate on *Talk to Her* instead. After winning his second Oscar, Almodóvar was convinced that he had to turn the script – now called *Bad Education* – which had been in development for more than three decades, into a film: 'I had to make it, to get it out of me before it became a frustrating obsession.' More than just an autobiographical experience, it was a very intimate story which exposed and denounced the sexual abuse that took place in religious schools and community centres: 'I'm not just telling a story about my school days [. . .] My memories were important when writing it, because, after all, I lived in the scenarios and in the times in which it takes place. But it is not about a settling of scores with the priests who miseducated me, nor with the clergy in general.'

LEFT: Father Manolo (Daniel Giménez Cacho), one of Almodóvar's most terrifying and irredeemable characters.

"THERE WAS A LOT OF ABUSE, ESPECIALLY AMONG THE YOUNGEST CHILDREN."

More than a vengeful work, *Bad Education* represents the filmmaker's umpteenth twist on the original concept of film noir. What, mistakenly, may seem to be an anticlerical drama by way of confession, is an arduous and splendid criminal game where cinema, specifically the figure of the tortured director who seeks to redeem himself through his art – already appreciated in *Law of Desire* and revisited in *Pain and Glory* – once again plays an essential role. Enrique (Fele Martínez) is a famous filmmaker who, one day in 1980, receives a mysterious visit from Ignacio (Gael García Bernal), an actor looking for work who claims to be an old schoolmate with whom he fell in love. He proposes to shoot a script he has written – curiously titled *The Visit* – about their years at their Catholic school, where they discovered their passion for cinema and suffered the abuses of Father Manolo (Daniel Giménez Cacho). But Enrique distrusts his old friend and ends up finding out that it is Ignacio's younger brother, Juan. Despite this, he agrees to direct the film in order to discover the truth about the fate of the real Ignacio.

From here, Almodóvar masterfully and delicately constructs a plot marked by a terrible murder and the passions that led to it. *Bad Education* is sprinkled with glorious noir references to *La Bête Humaine* (Jean Renoir, 1938) and *The Adultress* (*Thérèse Raquin*, Marcel Carné, 1953) and features an elemental archetype of the genre: the man with a dark past who becomes a femme fatale (Juan, transformed into the disconcerting Zahara), almost an heir to the transvestite murderer in *Dressed to Kill* (Brian De Palma, 1980). In this sense, the return to the Almodóvarian canon of cinematographer José Luis Alcaine is decisive. His use of colour again accompanies the moods of the characters and manages to create a diffuse and sombre atmosphere with the predominance of black, the tone that distinguishes the cassocks of the 'bad educators'.

Bad Education extends the look of *Talk to Her*, and similarly, is based on the connection between two men who are united by a traumatic event. This is Almodóvar's most masculine work, in terms of story and cast, and would require an exhaustive search throughout the Spanish-speaking acting world to find his longed-for leading man. Gael García Bernal was considered an international star when he was chosen for the role. Despite being only twenty-five years old, his career already included the award-winning *Amores perros* (Alejandro González Iñárritu, 2000) and *Y tu mamá también* (Alfonso Cuarón, 2001). Even so, he could not have imagined the demands Almodóvar would make of him during the almost four months of filming, starting with the obligatory neutralisation of his Mexican accent. He also had to learn some of the characteristic body language of the Spanish, taking flamenco classes, and studying the films of the camp icon Sara Montiel, as well as thoroughly reviewing the work of Carmen Maura and Victoria Abril in the director's earlier films. Despite acquiring all of these desired characteristics, García Bernal and Almodóvar maintained a very tense relationship throughout the production, to the point of stopping filming for a week so that the actor could recover emotionally.

His relationship with his other lead, Fele Martínez, was much smoother. He arrived already endorsed by his work with Alejandro Amenábar, Julio Medem and Jaume Balagueró, not forgetting his memorable contribution to *Talk to Her* as the tiny man in the fake silent film, *The Shrinking Lover*. 'I made him lose weight and train for five months until he got another body,' recalled the director. 'We also worked on his tone of voice; I lowered his vocal range. He put his heart and skin into it.' For the rest of the male roles, Almodóvar

ABOVE and LEFT: The reunion between Ángel and Enrique will be marked by uncontrollable passions, false identities and memories of a childhood of fear and discovery.

counted on experienced actors Daniel Giménez Cacho (a legend in Mexico thanks to his collaborations with Arturo Ripstein and Guillermo del Toro), Lluís Homar, who was reliably superb, and Javier Cámara, capable of bringing a touch of humour and tenderness to a tale of tragedy and doom.

Increasingly accustomed to shooting in places other than Madrid, Almodóvar moved his story to locations as diverse as Noia and the village of Ponte Nafonso (A Coruña), an impressive nineteenth-century neoclassical building in Alella (Barcelona), and the city of Valencia. In the latter city, several scenes were filmed in the neighbourhoods of El Carmen and Benimaclet, in addition to the legendary – but now defunct – Tyris cinema. In May 2004, *Bad Education* became the first Spanish film in history to open the Cannes Festival – a milestone that the filmmaker defined as 'the apogee of the honeymoon that I have been living with the French public for years' – just two months after its premiere in Spain, where it had a mixed reception, but ended up becoming a great box-office success, exceeding six million euros in earnings. Once again, the disconnect within the Spanish film industry when evaluating their most revered director (the film only received four Goya nominations, all without awards) would contrast with unanimous international acclaim, reflected in different nominations for the European Film Awards, the Césars, BAFTAs and the Independent Spirit Awards. Not even the protests of Catholic fundamentalists, who were consistently annoying and managed to stop the trailer for *Bad Education* from being screened in France before *The Passion of the Christ* (Mel Gibson, 2004), could overshadow its impressive reception.

ABOVE: Despite their reported differences, Almodóvar got Gael García Bernal to give one of the best and most disconcerting performances of his career.

RIGHT: Almodóvar demonstrates the position of a football goalkeeper to his young actor.

> IT IS NOT ABOUT A SETTLING OF SCORES WITH THE PRIESTS WHO MISEDUCATED ME.

VOLVER

VOLVER (2006)

In the first scene of *Bad Education*, Juan (Gael García Bernal) visits Enrique Goded's production company pretending to be his brother Ignacio. On the wall, next to the main door, there is a poster for a fictitious movie called *La abuela fantasma* (*The Ghostly Grandmother*), directed in the past by Enrique. What at first might seem to be just another element of the film's particular universe was in fact a foreshadowing from Almodóvar of his next project, which would end up being called *Volver* and would be, in effect, a return for the director to the common places of his cinema and his life: to the rural world of La Mancha, to comedy, to the indelible memory of his mother, to marginalized characters, to Penélope Cruz, to the cinema of fascinating women. A return even to Carmen Maura – the *ghostly grandmother* of this story – after eighteen years of personal and professional estrangement. 'It was very funny, because it had been a long time since we had seen each other,' recalled the actor. 'He called me and asked: "Do you mind playing a wreck?" And I told him: "What a question you are asking me. What's it going to matter to me?" Let's get along the way we get along; we both know the other one is doing well.'

Seen in perspective, *Volver* has become a work of key importance within Pedro Almodóvar's artistic output. It is a film full of warmth, tremendously tender and funny, in which the director presents some of his most unforgettable characters and illuminates them in a beautiful way. It is, in fact, a question of a continuous return, a reunion with his origins after a particularly intense dramatic journey. It is no coincidence that *Volver* is a film twinned with *The Flower of My Secret*, the 1995 title that Almodóvar wrote and shot to make up for such turbulent stories as *Tie Me Up! Tie Me Down!*, *High Heels* and *Kika*. In both we find a woman undergoing a vital transformation, let down once again by a man, who decides to return to her village home and reconnect with her mother to find a new meaning to her existence. Almodóvar himself acknowledges that the initial idea for *Volver* came from the crime novel written by *The Flower of My Secret*'s Leo Macías (Marisa Paredes), in which a woman murders her daughter's father to protect her and then hides the corpse in the cold storage room of a restaurant.

In Almodóvar's mind, there was never any other Raimunda than Penélope Cruz. The actor from Madrid gives a prodigious performance in *Volver* and becomes one of the bravest and most charming women in the filmmaker's imagination, inspired by the Sophia Loren of the early years, with Claudia Cardinale's hairstyle and the imposing physical presence and working-class beauty of Anna Magnani in Luchino Visconti's *Bellissima*. 'I wanted Penélope to be inspired by the great Mediterranean icons of acting, very physical, visceral women, with all the emotions on the surface, so obvious, vulgar and uninhibited. Fortunately for her, that's just the way she usually approaches and embodies her characters.'

Like Gloria in *What Have I Done to Deserve This?*, Raimunda lives on the outskirts of Madrid and works hard to provide for her daughter, Paula (Yohana Cobo), while her husband, Paco (Antonio de la Torre), dedicates himself to being lazy and feeding his vices and perversions.

LEFT: *Volver* was a glorious return to suburban comedy, to the traditions of La Mancha and, above all, to the stories of radiant, feisty women.

I WANTED PENÉLOPE TO BE INSPIRED BY THE GREAT MEDITERRANEAN ICONS OF ACTING, VERY PHYSICAL, VISCERAL WOMEN, WITH ALL THE EMOTIONS ON THE SURFACE.

LEFT: In her third film with Almodóvar, Penélope Cruz plays a woman of overflowing charisma, based on the great Italian actresses of the 1950s.

RIGHT: The performance of the film's title song is undoubtedly one of *Volver*'s highlights.

Like Gloria's character, her life is turned upside down when circumstances force Paula to kill her father to protect herself, and Raimunda must use her wits to get rid of the body. Because of this, she's unable to return to her childhood home for her aunt's funeral, but her sister, Sole (Lola Dueñas), is able to go. After the funeral, her aunt's neighbour, Agustina (Blanca Portillo), tells Sole that she overheard her aunt talking to her dead mother's ghost. When she returns to Madrid, Sole discovers that this ghost of her mother (Carmen Maura), who died in a fire years ago, is also travelling in her car. Rather than look for a logical explanation, Sole accepts that she must live with her, and even puts her to work in her lover's hairdressers, posing as a Russian tramp. 'I wanted the dead mother to be present in her daughters' lives as a physical ghost, with the same needs as a human being,' explained the director. 'Here, the ghost only shows herself to Sole, who is the most gullible and easily manipulated of the sisters. According to the traditional superstition of La Mancha, ghosts return to this world to solve things they left unfinished in life. That is the intention of the mother's ghost.'

Almodóvar sets up a brilliant conflict between the sisters and what they hide from each other. While Raimunda lies to hide Paco's death, Sole does the same to cover up the fact that her mother has come back to life.

HAIRDRESSER'S CLIENT: **Sole, what about the Russian?**

RAIMUNDA: **Who's the Russian?**

SOLE: **I have one here to help me.**

CLIENT: **Yes, well, I was just telling her about my Borja, who's been given another expulsion warning. What do you think? He's punctured the tyres of the priest who teaches him religion. . . Well, I'm telling her about it, and she leaves me there alone, talking, and with my hair half washed.**

SOLE: **She must have gone out.**

CLIENT: **It's not that she's gone out. . . She ran away.**

SOLE: **She suffers from claustrophobia, and sometimes the poor woman needs to go outside.**

RAIMUNDA: **Well, what a help. And you pay her for that?**

SOLE: **No. I keep her at home. She eats and sleeps here. I've given her Mum's clothes.**

RAIMUNDA: **I don't like you picking up people you don't know, Sole.**

CLIENT: **We've told her. . . That she's too nice and people take advantage of her. Look at the Russian. You can't imagine how she lives here. Like a queen.**

SOLE: **And Paco? How did it go the other night?**

RAIMUNDA: **Very bad. He came home to get his clothes. . . I think he's living with another woman now. But come on, I don't know where he is, and I don't care. Hey, why didn't you tell me you had a Russian woman here?**

SOLE: **I must have forgotten, I don't know.**

As a child, Almodóvar was impressed by the traditional La Mancha ritual of women cleaning gravestones in the cemetery. Paradoxically, in *Volver* he chose it as the opening sequence. 'Now I look at death with less strangeness, in a more natural way, with more serenity. More than a film about death itself, *Volver* is about the rich culture that surrounds it in the place where I was born. It is about the way (not at all tragic) that several female characters, from different generations, must face this reality,' he said, about the way in which the film naturalises this issue until it is an accepted part of life, stripping it of any transcendence. 'When my grandfather died, he left many things unresolved. Then he appeared to a brother-in-law of his, who became ill from the apparitions. Until one day the women told him not to be afraid, to ask the ghost what he wanted. The thing is so incredible that eventually the whole town accompanied my grandfather's brother-in-law and my grandfather's spirit to the cemetery to say goodbye to him. I think that image of a procession accompanying a ghost is just great.'

In the case of these sisters, death arrives to provide solace to the empty and isolated Sole – her full name, appropriately enough, being Soledad, meaning loneliness – and as a motivator and self-affirmation for Raimunda, through getting a job at the same restaurant where she was forced to hide her husband's corpse. This is the main theme of the film – and a recurring one in many of Almodóvar's films, but by no means the only one: the importance of roots, the bond with the mother, the strength of character in the face of adversity, and female camaraderie (represented by the wonderful Agustina, the neighbour who is always there when needed) all make *Volver* a true celebration of the genius and passion of a filmmaker at the height of his powers.

Between July and September 2005, Almodóvar moved the production from the Madrid neighbourhoods of Tetuán and Vallecas to various towns and villages in his beloved Castilla-La Mancha: Granátula, Calzada and Valenzuela amongst them. But it was in Almagro, famous for its beautiful historic centre made up of palaces, churches, ancestral homes and the Corral de Comedias (built during the Spanish Golden Age), that the director found the traditional Manchegan home that would house Agustina (Blanca Portillo), not far from the location that a decade earlier had hosted several scenes in *The Flower of My Secret*. 'I love the austerity of its streets, the cobblestones, the black iron windows, without flowerpots, clean of any kind of ornamentation. The dark plinth. The intense daylight,' said Almodóvar during filming. Even the music composed by Alberto Iglesias is once again rich with that Hispanic nuance absent from the director's more recent films, resorting to a string quartet, Spanish guitar and a main theme that borrows pasodoble traits. Not forgetting, of course, the inclusion of Carlos Gardel's iconic tango from the sublime and deep voice of Estrella Morente.

Almost two decades after its release, *Volver* remains Almodóvar's biggest box-office success in Spain, with more than ten million euros grossed and an audience of almost two million. It was one of the rare instances in the director's career in which the audience, critics and academics were all in agreement: not even the reticent Goyas could resist its magnetism, awarding it a total of five awards, including Best Film, Director and Actress. Outside Spain, the reception was equally passionate, demonstrating that only Almodóvar could produce a film with such universal resonance from a story so intimate and rooted in a particular country and culture. With a global box office of $85 million, it is the second-highest-grossing film in Spanish history – only surpassed by the Mexican *Instructions Not Included* (*No se aceptan devoluciones*, Eugenio Derbez, 2013) – and its accolades included four European Film Awards, two awards at Cannes (Best Screenplay and Best Actress for the entire female ensemble) and an Oscar nomination for Penélope Cruz, the first Spanish actor to achieve this distinction.

ABOVE LEFT: Carmen Maura and Penélope Cruz, the two great and undisputed muses of Almodóvar's cinema.

ABOVE RIGHT: The film was Maura's first work with the director since 1988.

LEFT: Lola Dueñas, in the centre of the picture, brings all her candour and comic talent to the character of Sole.

NEXT PAGE: The cemeteries of La Mancha are one of the most symbolic locations in the film.

TOMAS

MORE THAN A FILM ABOUT DEATH ITSELF, *VOLVER* IS ABOUT THE RICH CULTURE THAT SURROUNDS IT.

BROKEN EMBRACES

BROKEN EMBRACES

Los abrazos rotos (2009)

Pedro Almodóvar's seventeenth film is the story of two embraces, one real and furtive, the other cinematographic. The first was captured by the director's own camera in 1999, in Lanzarote's Playa del Golfo, during a vacation on the island shortly after the death of his mother. 'That visit happened at a very special time,' he recalled. 'My spirit, still in mourning, found a reflection and a comfort in the blackness of the island, like a kind of energy shot.' One day, he decided to photograph the immense black volcanic sands of a beach without noticing that, hidden in the distant landscape, a couple were passionately embracing. When he saw the developed image, Almodóvar began to imagine their lives, trying to find out the reasons for that fleeting gesture. He tried to find them, without success, but from then, he knew he would make a film about an almost secret embrace, in that same place, surrounded by the dramatic and captivating nature of the island.

The filmmaker returned to the dramatic landscape of Lanzarote several times, trying to find the inspiration to finish the story, but none of the ideas met his expectations. However, in the early months of 2007, a succession of severe migraines forced him to cancel a trip to New York to write a script with Paul Auster, and to lock himself in a darkened room for several days. It was in this blackness that Almodóvar discovered the way to tell the story that had proved so elusive to him: through the figure of a blind director, someone who was once immensely happy but whose embraces were cut short by a fateful destiny.

'I felt that it is the first time that I had made such an express declaration of love for cinema, not with a specific scene, but with

RIGHT: Almodóvar's irresistible metacinema: Carmen Machi and Penélope Cruz in a scene from *Chicas y maletas*, the film within the film.

the whole film,' explained Almodóvar. The film once again centres around a film director, played by Lluís Homar – the third film director, though not the last, to feature in one of Almodóvar's films, after *Law of Desire* and *Bad Education*. 'It is a statement about something that, even if you can make a living from it, is not just a profession, but an irrational passion.' Indeed, *Broken Embraces* is probably his most kaleidoscopic work as far as the device of 'cinema within cinema' is concerned, and the one that focuses most clearly on the gaze of the filmmaker, marked by tragedy. Everything, from the photograph on the beach to the darkness of blindness, is part of a unique and particular perspective in which Almodóvar makes the viewers participants.

The second embrace references, once again, a cinematic memory. There is a scene where Mateo Blanco (Lluís Homar) and Lena (Penélope Cruz) watch *Journey to Italy* (*Viaggio in Italia*, Roberto Rossellini, 1954) on television, one of the masterpieces of neorealism. In that film, a couple, played by Ingrid Bergman and George Sanders, visit Pompeii and come across a shocking scene: the petrified bodies of a woman and a man, immortalised by the lava of Vesuvius while they slept two thousand years ago. In that instant, Bergman's character, and by extension Penélope's, are moved by this demonstration of a love so strong it is capable of resisting death itself. Lena feels the urge to embrace Mateo, to hold him close to her in the face of adversity and decides to preserve that moment with a photograph that, shortly afterwards, will end up broken into a thousand pieces.

LEFT: Almodóvar makes the final adjustments to a shot of Penélope Cruz in front of a mirror...

RIGHT: ... and runs through some dialogue with Tamar Novas and Lluís Homar.

LENA: **What are you writing?**
MATEO: **'The secret of Playa del Golfo.' When I took the photo, I didn't see the couple kissing.**
LENA: **And what is their secret?**
MATEO: **I don't know. I have to write it down to find out.**
LENA: **That couple is us.**

Broken Embraces is one of the most complex stories to emerge from Almodóvar's mind. A challenge that the director felt he could only take on based on the artistic recognition that had accompanied him during the last decade, and that placed him, on his own merits, in a privileged situation from which to face such a risky project. At any other stage in his career, or in the hands of any other author, a film so marked by fatality, so intricate and demanding on the page, would have been a leap into the void with unpredictable consequences. Instead, Almodóvar masterfully solves the challenge and creates a labyrinthine plot in which the characters, and the narrative itself, develop a constant duplicity: two eras (1994

“IT IS THE FIRST TIME THAT I HAD MADE SUCH AN EXPRESS DECLARATION OF LOVE FOR CINEMA, NOT WITH A SPECIFIC SCENE, BUT WITH THE WHOLE FILM.”

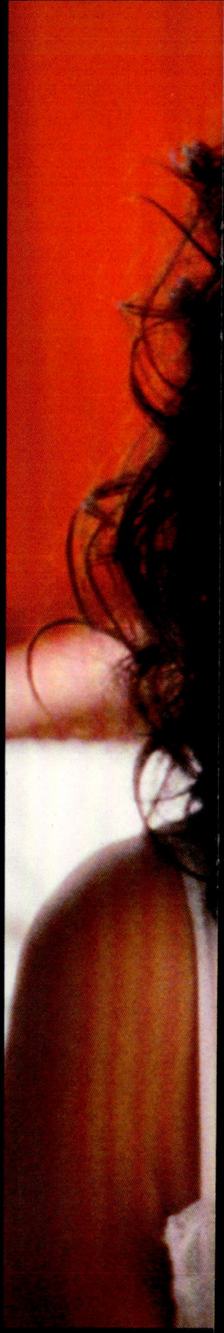

and the present), a lead character split into two personalities (Mateo Blanco, the brilliant filmmaker, and Harry Caine, the disgraced screenwriter, blind after the car accident that killed his beloved), two Ernesto Martels (father and son, one arrived to destroy and the other to rebuild) and even two different plot lines, that of the story itself – the reality – and that of the film shot by the director – the fiction.

Almodóvar loved filming the scenes for this fake film, titled *Chicas y maletas* (*Girls and Suitcases*) and inspired by the frenetic surrealism of *Women on the Verge of a Nervous Breakdown*: 'We shot it in the exact same spot in the studio where we made the original, twenty years earlier. I had a lot of fun adapting myself, it was a very inspiring experience.' This is a new and splendid demonstration of cinematographic metalanguage by the director, probably the only one capable of extracting a passage full of sublime comedy – where neither the suitcase nor the *gazpacho* so characteristic of the 1988 film are missing – from such a decidedly cruel and stormy context. Undoubtedly, the great attraction of *Girls and Suitcases* is the conservative-minded council member, Chon, played by Carmen Machi, a cyclonic woman fond of sex, drugs and cannibalism. Almodóvar was so taken with the character that he ended up shooting more scenes than the film required, which gave rise to an eight-minute short film, *La concejala antropófaga* (*The Cannibalistic Councillor*), in which the

ABOVE: Lena (Penélope Cruz) feels trapped in a life she no longer wants.

> A TRUE POET OF CINEMA, SOMEONE WHO CREATES TERRIBLE AND HEALING IMAGES THAT LIVE IN YOUR HEAD AS IF IN A WAKING DREAM.
>
> *ROLLING STONE*

LEFT: Except for her brief appearance in *I'm So Excited!*, *Broken Embraces* is the only Almodóvar film in which Penélope Cruz's character does not have to deal with problematic motherhood.

origin of her depraved dietary habits is riotously disclosed.

Almodóvar began production of *Broken Embraces* in Lanzarote at the end of May 2008. The crew stayed for two weeks, working in various locations: Famara beach, the volcanic and vineyard area of La Geria, Charco de Los Clicos, Timanfaya National Park and the village of Tahíche, which was chosen for the car accident scenes and where, in 1992 (in a coincidence unknown to Almodóvar), the admired Canarian artist César Manrique had died. Filming continued at Madrid's Barajas studios and at other locations around the city, such as an apartment on Cuenca Street, owned by the director's sister, which had already been used for several scenes for *The Flower of My Secret*. The shoot – one of the most arduous and ambitious of Almodóvar's career – was supported by one of the best cinematographers in the world, the Mexican Rodrigo Prieto, used regularly by Alejandro González Iñarritu and Martin Scorsese, and a specialist in achieving textures shrouded in darkness. In addition, the filmmaker brought together a cast made up of many of his usual accomplices: Blanca Portillo, Ángela Molina, Kiti Mánver and Lola Dueñas. However, his relationship with his lead actor Lluís Homar was tense throughout, with the actor claiming to have felt insecure in such a demanding role and due to the director's apparent disappointment in his performance. The fall-out was such that he was totally ignored by Almodóvar after shooting and had no role in the promotion of the film. The film was released in Spain in March 2009, with Almodóvar buoyed by a succession of triumphant works and Penélope Cruz having just won an Oscar for her performance in *Vicky Cristina Barcelona* (Woody Allen, 2008), but the unexpected happened. At the box office, its gross was less than half that of *Volver*, with only a third of the audience, and it received scathing reviews from some critics. It even underperformed in those countries – France and the USA – usually so loyal to the director, although internationally it ended up garnering endless praise from the most prestigious publications. While *The Wall Street Journal* spoke of a 'totally delicious' film, *Variety* highlighted 'the extraordinary strength of the cinematic personality' of its director, who was described by *Rolling Stone* magazine as 'a true poet of cinema, someone who creates terrible and healing images that live in your head as if in a waking dream.'

THE SKIN I LIVE IN

ABOVE: Elena Anaya (Vera) and Antonio Banderas (Ledgard) listen to Almodóvar's instructions before shooting one of the most powerful scenes in the film.

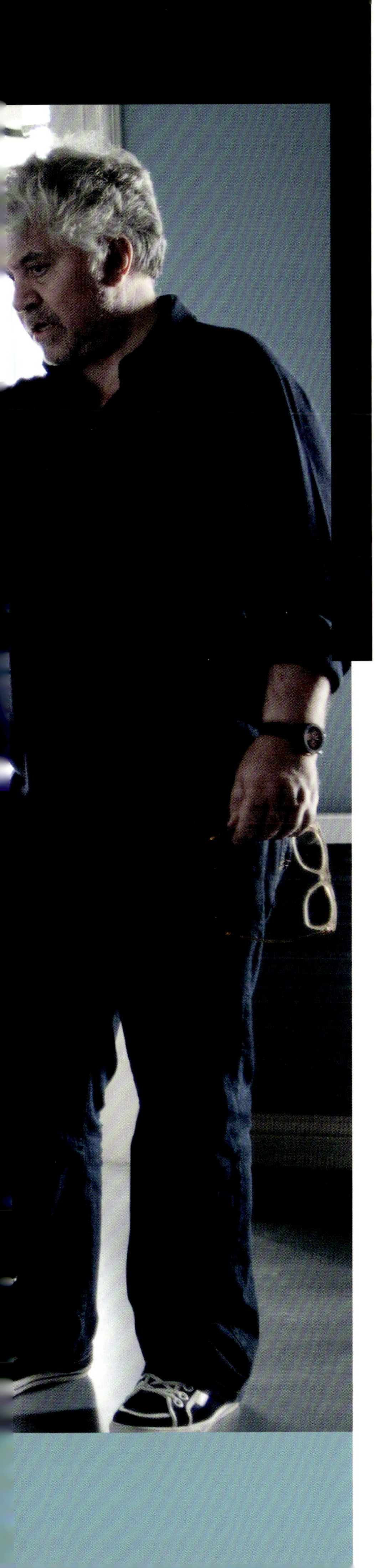

THE SKIN I LIVE IN

La piel que habito (2011)

Like many projects in Almodóvar's career, *The Skin I Live In* underwent a long development period and multiple transformations. At the beginning of the twenty-first century, fresh from the international success of *All About My Mother*, the director had been fascinated by the 1984 novel *Tarantula*, by the great French master of noir literature Thierry Jonquet. After acquiring the film rights through El Deseo, Almodóvar began writing nearly twenty versions of the script, none of which convinced him. 'I worked on the story for nine years,' he says, of a process full of uncertainties during which he even considered shooting a silent, black-and-white adaptation, as a kind of tribute to his idols Fritz Lang and F. W. Murnau, with cards on which the key plot elements and dialogue would appear. 'After hesitating for months, I decided to go my own way and let myself be carried away by intuition – which after all is what I have always done – without the shadow of the masters of the genre and renouncing my own cinematographic memory.'

The fact that the script didn't adhere to any one specific genre – it lies somewhere between noir, science fiction and horror – was a headache for Almodóvar when defining the film's approach. 'I wrote it many times because, when I got to the end, there was always something I didn't like. To tell the truth, the most sensible thing would have been to abandon it. When a script gives you so many problems that you always seem to get stuck, maybe it's because it has no solution. But, as I was still very interested in the central situation of the story, I kept thinking about it until I finally found the solution.' Finally, the only element that Almodóvar kept from Jonquet's novel was the protagonist's desire for revenge. Robert Ledgard is a renowned plastic surgeon obsessed with the tragic death of his wife after suffering severe burns in an accident, and so invents an artificial skin incapable of being damaged.

Back on his own creative terrain, the La Mancha-born filmmaker knew how to imbue the story with his unmistakable stamp. As had already happened with his previous literary adaptation (*Live Flesh*), he made so many modifications that his personality ended up absorbing the original material almost in its entirety. Thus, the viewer is reunited with entirely identifiable Almodóvarian archetypes, from the two-faced psychopath of *Matador* to the love-blinded kidnapper (and his captive victim) of *Tie Me Up! Tie Me Down!*, touching on characteristic themes of his universe such as transsexuality, self-destruction, atonement and loss. While the representation of motherhood acquires the tragic component of titles such as *High Heels* or *All About My Mother*, the character of Marilia (the superb Marisa Paredes) must deal with a suffocating sense of guilt, and with the certainty of having given birth to two very different incarnations of evil, Ledgard and Zeca, while hoping for a spiritual redemption that never arrives. As in *Bad Education*, the shadow of Cain and Abel hovers over the brothers, and one of them even appears dressed as a tiger, giving rise to a

contrast as trashy and grotesque as that which, three decades earlier, was caused by the presence of that same animal among the nuns of *Dark Habits*.

The Skin I Live In marked Almodóvar's reunion with the crime genre, and with Antonio Banderas, twenty-one years after their last collaboration (which, coincidentally, also revolved around an unstable individual who holds a young woman against her will in his home). It feels fitting that their paths should meet again at the height of their careers, one as the director revered around the world, the other as an undisputed star of Hollywood. 'I was eager to work with Antonio again, but we had to wait for the right vehicle,' said the director, who during rehearsals had to ask his leading man to shed his acting tics, as he was looking for a very restrained character, while Banderas initially planned to tackle the role of Dr. Robert Ledgard as a stereotypical film psychopath. 'He was very prepared, but I explained to him that, although I like very baroque characters, the story was so fantastical that even with the slightest hint of over-acting we would go too far. So, I insisted until I emptied his face of any emotion.' For the actor, the experience meant a return to Almodóvar's discipline after two decades of very different jobs in the United States: 'When it comes to Pedro, the shortest distance between two points is never a straight line. Shooting with him is anything but boring. In America we actors enjoy a lot of freedom, but this is unthinkable in his cinema. He directs you in a very specific way, he doesn't allow ideas. But when you let him guide you, everything goes very well.'

Almodóvar contrasts Ledgard's implacable voracity with the apparent fragility and subtlety of his victim, Lena, a young woman who has been trapped for six years for an unknown reason, beyond serving as a human guinea pig for her captor's terrible experiments.

LEFT: The director goes over the script with Marisa Paredes (Marilia) and Roberto Álamo (Zeca), Zera's mother and criminal brother.

LENA: **Do you like what you see?**

LEDGARD: **What do you mean?**

LENA: **Is there something you want to improve?**

LEDGARD: **No. I don't want to improve anything.**

LENA: **Then I can consider myself complete?**

LEDGARD: **Yes. And you can boast of having the best skin in the world.**

LENA: **What now?**

LEDGARD: **Now I'm going to light this opium ball, and I'm going to smoke it.**

LENA: **I mean us. I mean me. If I'm finished... What are you going to do with me?**

LEDGARD: **I don't know. I'll think about it.**

LENA: **When?**

LEDGARD: **If you keep asking, I'm leaving.**

LENA: **Don't you think the simplest thing would be to live? To live together?**

LEDGARD: **Live together? How?**

LENA: **Like everybody else.**

LEDGARD: **You and I are not like everybody else.**

LENA: **Look at it as another one of your experiments... Living together as equals [...] I'm yours. I'm tailor-made for you. And you just told me you like me.**

LEDGARD: **Did I say that?**

LENA: **I know you look at me. Since you brought me here, we practically live in the same room.**

Although Penélope Cruz was originally attached to play Lena, the role was eventually given to Elena Anaya, a wonderful dramatic actor who had previously worked with the director in a small role in *Talk to Her*. 'Pedro is very affectionate, obsessive about perfection and detail-oriented,' she said. 'It is true that he directs the actors a lot, but he also gives you the key you need and that, in turn, coincides with what he is looking for in each shot.' Lena is the great mystery of *The Skin I Live In*, someone who hides a devastating secret and has a special bond with her fellow captive Vicente (Jan Cornet), who was involved long ago in the tragic death of Ledgard's daughter. To strengthen their characters' chemistry, Anaya and Cornet began spending time off-set together without Almodóvar's knowledge, and even went jogging at the same time so that their bodies would naturally synchronise. Their efforts were rewarded when, during filming, the director noticed that both walked in a very similar way and congratulated them on it.

PEDRO IS VERY AFFECTIONATE, OBSESSIVE ABOUT PERFECTION AND DETAIL-ORIENTED.

ELENA ANAYA

ABOVE: Elena Anaya's extraordinary and highly complex performance brought her several awards, including the Goya Award for Best Actress.

BELOW: After several unsuccessful attempts, Banderas and Almodóvar returned to work together, ending a long hiatus of more than two decades.

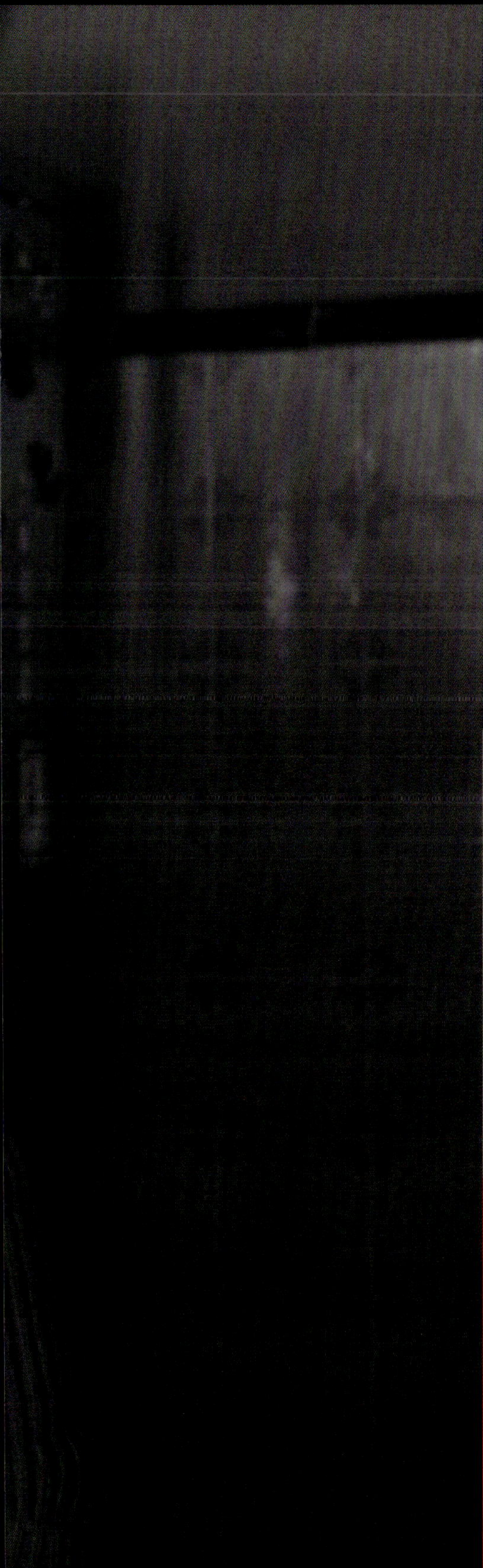

WHEN IT COMES TO PEDRO, THE SHORTEST DISTANCE BETWEEN TWO POINTS IS NEVER A STRAIGHT LINE. SHOOTING WITH HIM IS ANYTHING BUT BORING.

ANTONIO BANDERAS

The film had a budget of ten million euros and was shot mainly in an eighteenth-century manor house in Toledo, with some scenes set in Santiago de Compostela and the Pazo de Oca (Pontevedra). As he had done on other occasions (remember, for example, the extraordinary fusion of film, literature and dance in *The Flower of My Secret*), Almodóvar gave free rein to his artistic spirit with a dazzling combination of disciplines, from the sculptures of Louise Bourgeois – Lena's great inspiration during her confinement – to the multitude of art distributed throughout the house – Titian, Juan Gatti and Guillermo Pérez Villalta, among others – passing through the different versions of *Frankenstein* and *Pygmalion*. Alberto Iglesias based his majestic score on the ballet piece *Cautiva*, composed by himself for the film *¡Dispara!* (Carlos Saura, 1993) and with clear references to the work of masters such as Bernard Herrmann or Jerry Goldsmith. Not to mention the film influences, which include gems of the calibre of *The Invisible Man* (James Whale, 1933), *Rebecca* (Alfred Hitchcock, 1940), *Eyes Without a Face* (Georges Franju, 1960) and even *The Silence of the Lambs* (Jonathan Demme, 1991), where a psychopath creates a second skin, flayed from his victims, to satisfy his need to change sex.

Like *Broken Embraces*, *The Skin I Live In* was received rapturously by critics but with a certain lack of enthusiasm by the public, who were disconcerted by the oppressive and dark tone of Almodóvar's latest work. In Spain, the film barely grossed more than four million euros. Time, however, has been kind to the film, which is now considered an exquisite and sombre rarity.

I'M SO EXCITED!

I'M SO EXCITED!

Los amantes pasajeros (2013)

I'm So Excited! came about as a reaction to a debt Almodóvar felt he owed to his audience. 'When I walked down the street, they would always tell me the same thing: that they loved my latest films, how much I had matured with those dramas. . . But then they would remind me how much they had laughed with me, and I felt a huge responsibility.' Aware that his fans had long been calling for a return to his irreverent and crazy comedies of the eighties, he decided to give in to their wishes and dusted off a half-written script about a group of quirky characters travelling on a flight between Madrid and Mexico City. The grotesque characters include a corrupt businessman, a VIP dominatrix, a hired killer, a psychic, a failed actor, an engaged couple and a peculiar trio of cabin crew with a liking for narcotics. 'Many of the plots of my films, or new ideas that break a narrative logjam if that's the case, have occurred to me while travelling by plane, surrounded by strangers,' Almodóvar said, of the inspirational role that these journeys have always played in his films.

'The idea came to me very early on, and I wrote the first half feverishly, as a comic whim,' he recalls. 'What I found difficult was to finish it off so that it wouldn't turn out to be a banal exercise, funny but superfluous. Comedy demands a certain reflection of reality, even if it is hidden among the humour of the situations.' That *reality* of which Almodóvar spoke referred to the protest movement known as 15-M, initiated in May 2011 in Spain by different social organisations that demanded a profound change in a system marked by political corruption and an unsustainable economic situation. *I'm So Excited!* was a response to the need felt by the director to raise his voice in solidarity with the protests in his own way. The passengers represent a microcosm of society, with all of its lies, divisions and moral degradation, with the masses represented in the anaesthetised tourist class, while the middle classes sit in business unable to give up their privileges. In this way, a film initially conceived as a broad comedy becomes, against the odds, a paradigm of social awareness: 'I don't want to say that it is prophetic, but when there are social upheavals – and we are now living through the strongest I can remember since democracy – films can become old or, on the contrary, acquire

ABOVE: With *I'm So Excited!*, Almodóvar returned to the ensemble and crazed comedy of *Women on the Verge of a Nervous Breakdown*.

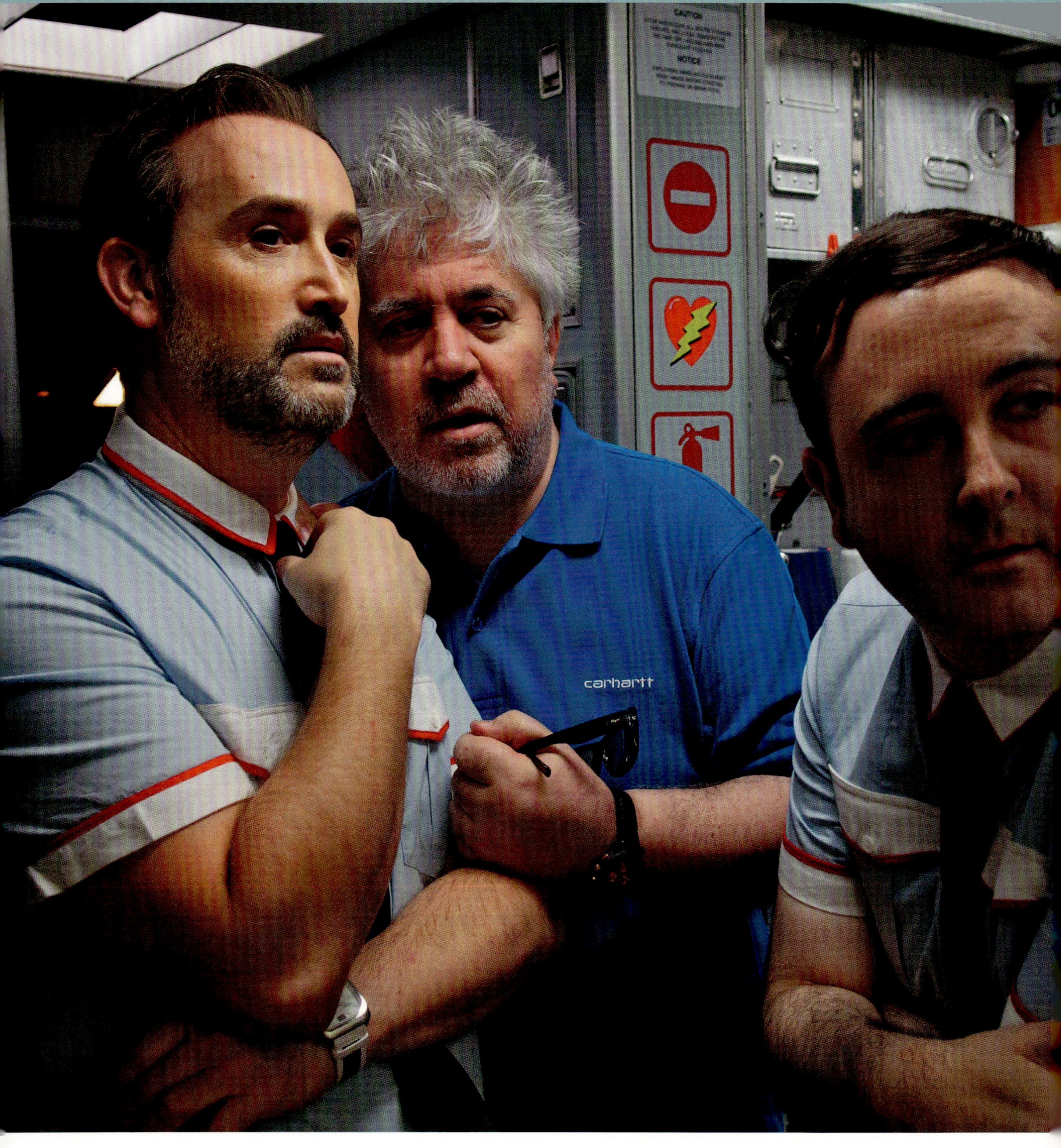
CAUTION
NOTICE
carhartt

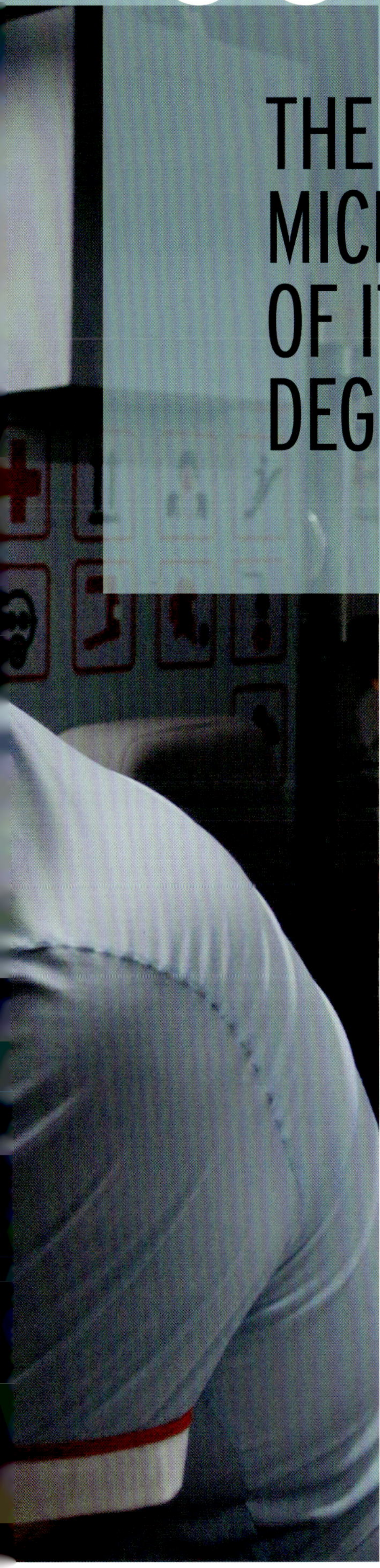

> **THE PASSENGERS REPRESENT A MICROCOSM OF SOCIETY, WITH ALL OF ITS LIES, DIVISIONS AND MORAL DEGRADATION.**

a dimension in an unconscious way, a meaning that was not in the director's head.'

It is not difficult to draw a clear comparison between a country on the brink of revolution and a faulty aeroplane: both seem doomed to crash due to their own negligence. When a technical problem forces a Peninsula Airbus to circle over Spain awaiting an emergency landing, the passengers and crew believe they are about to die and decide to indulge in their innermost confessions and their most unattainable fantasies. 'During the gestation of the film there was no conscious cinematic reference; in fact, theatre, television, and my own claustrophobia are more present than cinema. To tell the truth, my films owe a lot to theatre, they are full of scenes with two performers, sometimes of undisguised monologues,' admitted Almodóvar, who was especially seduced by the idea of having a group locked up and devoid of any technology, whose only recourse is the words they share with each other. 'They relate to one another, they unburden themselves, lie, assume they have lied, seduce and are seduced, and thus they can fight against fear, loneliness and the idea of death.'

Only an artist of the magnitude and confidence of Almodóvar could enclose some of the most renowned performers of Spanish cinema – none with a leading role in such a choral story – to film in a single and very limited space, during the summer months and with temperatures that, at times, approached fifty degrees due to the heat of the spotlights. There, in complete harmony, we find old acquaintances of the director, such as Javier Cámara, Lola Dueñas, Antonio de la Torre and Cecilia Roth, who received the script shortly before embarking on a theatrical tour of Argentina, which she hastily gave up for the opportunity to work with Almodóvar again, fourteen years after *All About My Mother*. Alongside them are new additions: Hugo Silva, Miguel Ángel Silvestre, Guillermo Toledo, José María Yazpik, José Luis Torrijo, Raúl Arévalo and Carlos Areces, whose instinct for comedy turned his character, Fajas, into someone much more Machiavellian than the script

LEFT: The director, pictured here with Javier Cámara (Joserra) and Carlos Areces (Fajas), faced the logistical challenge of shooting on a set that reproduced the interior of an aeroplane.

LEFT: Almodóvar places the lens behind his admired Cecilia Roth (Norma).

RIGHT: Blanca Suárez (Ruth), one of the few stars of the film whose scenes take place on dry land.

suggested, a development that pleased the director enormously. The few scenes that take place outside the aircraft featured brief but stellar appearances by Paz Vega, Carmen Machi and Blanca Suárez, as well as two Almodóvarian icons, Antonio Banderas and Penélope Cruz, together for the first time in one of his films.

With *I'm So Excited!*, Almodóvar decided to shoot the film in Castilla-La Mancha, not because he wanted once again to show the traditions and idiosyncrasies of its inhabitants, but because the local airport, Ciudad Real, was then disused and had all the necessary infrastructure for filming. Inside a huge warehouse, the film crew took thirteen weeks to build a full-scale aircraft, which could be disassembled to facilitate camera movements, with parts acquired on the second-hand market and imported from Germany.

Once the sets were built, the technicians, actors and the director filmed for almost two months in the confined space offered by the cabin, while cinematographer José Luis Alcaine battled to keep the lights out of shot. In order to encourage the cast to bond under the harsh conditions of the production, El Deseo built a colourful little village next door, which they called Little Miami. There, the stars of the film each had a dressing room, a communal rest area with a ping-pong table, and an impressive catering service to help them cope with the long work sessions. 'We were all very

attentive to our colleagues, and in the end, we formed a real group of people supporting each other,' said Lola Dueñas. 'Even if we didn't have to be in the shot, we were always there to give feedback.'

For its international distribution, the film changed its title to *I'm So Excited!* – the Spanish title was a pun on *Passing Lovers* and *Loving Passengers* – in reference to the song by the Pointer Sisters that led to one of the film's funniest scenes, in which the three cabin crew perform a flamboyant dance to the track. In Spain, the film got off to a flying start, with the best opening weekend figures ever for an Almodóvar film: an audience of 250,000 and a gross of €1.86 million. However, mixed reviews caused a fifty-five per cent drop in its second week, leaving the final box office at just over €5 million, far from the numbers achieved by earlier films such as *Volver*, *All About My Mother* or *Talk to Her*. Something similar happened in most foreign markets too, where audience opinions were divided, leading to a commercial performance below expectations, except in France.

JULIETA

JULIETA (2016)

When Almodóvar filmed the scene in *The Skin I Live In* in which Marilia (Marisa Paredes) puts a copy of *Runaway* on her prisoner's breakfast tray, he was already working on the adaptation of three short stories from the book, written by Canadian author and Nobel Prize laureate Alice Munro. Although these stories, entitled 'Chance,' 'Soon' and 'Silence', were independent of each other, they had the same protagonist and a series of common themes (love, the passage of time, separation) that, in a way, grouped them together. An accurate portraitist – like Munro herself – of female idiosyncrasy, Almodóvar acquired the rights to the book in 2009 and turned the three narratives into a single story that straddled two eras: 'They were not consecutive, but I wanted to unify them by inventing whatever was necessary.'

It was to be the first film that Almodóvar would write and shoot entirely in English, having previously declined proposals as seductive as *Brokeback Mountain* – turned into a contemporary classic by Ang Lee – or an adaptation of Irène Némirovsky's novel *Suite française*. Feeling an affinity to the American way of life rather than to the Canadian one, he relocated the action of Munro's book from Vancouver to Boston first, and then to New York, delving into a family model unknown to him but very similar in both countries, where parents and children separate at very early ages and the distance between them, in most cases, is not only emotional but also geographical. However, with pre-production already underway and Meryl Streep lined up to play the lead, the director decided to back out and put the project on hold. 'I was defeated by uncertainty. I didn't feel confident about the script or my ability to work in English; I speak it well enough to direct the actors, but I'm referring to the *idea*. I feared having to change language, culture and country. So, I kept the first draft, which I had written in Spanish, without any specific plan for it.'

In 2014, a year after the premiere of *I'm So Excited!*, Almodóvar travelled to the Algarve in Portugal, accompanied by two of his closest collaborators, with the intention of mapping out what his next project would be. They reminded him how much they had liked that initial adaptation of Munro's book and suggested that he move the story to Spain. The director loved the idea and soon had a new version ready, in which the author's original concept was diluted in a typically Spanish and Almodóvarian context: 'I chose to follow my own way and

RIGHT: In *Julieta*, Adriana Ugarte took on a huge dramatic commitment, and put herself completely in Almodóvar's hands to build the character.

ABOVE: The director embraces Ugarte after a shot of great emotional intensity.

forget about Munro. I had to fly with my own wings. It was like the moment when teenagers leave their parents behind and take charge of their own lives.' In the end, Almodóvar had introduced so many changes – especially in the denouement – and had integrated the story into his universe in such a meticulous way, that what began as a free adaptation ended up becoming a tribute where the initial inspiration almost vanished. As in his previous literary translations (*Live Flesh* and *The Skin I Live In*), only the original concept was retained. This time not even the reference remained, since Almodóvar had chosen to use the title of one of the three stories ('Silence') but was forced to change it when he discovered that Martin Scorsese was working on a film with the same name, also scheduled for release in 2016.

Its stark exploration of loneliness and loss and the conflict between mothers and daughters makes *Julieta* the filmmaker's most painful film, and the only one in which he does not resort to humour as a palliative element. Nor is there a mix of genres: everything is pure drama, with Bergman as an invisible guest. 'It's a very different movie from the rest,' he says. 'I imposed sobriety and restraint during each day of the shoot. It was deliberate.' Unlike *Broken Embraces*, in which Lluís Homar played both a young and mature version of

“ITS STARK EXPLORATION OF LONELINESS AND LOSS AND THE CONFLICT BETWEEN MOTHERS AND DAUGHTERS MAKES *JULIETA* THE FILMMAKER’S MOST PAINFUL FILM.”

his character, Almodóvar wanted two different actors to represent the different stages of Julieta's life. Emma Suárez would play her in the present, when the character's hidden suffering reappears due to an encounter with an old friend of her daughter's from whom she has been estranged for years. We then meet the Julieta from 1985 (Adriana Ugarte), see her fiery encounter on a train with a fisherman named Xoan (Daniel Grao) and the tragic event that will forever change the lives of Julieta and her little girl, Antía.

XOAN **(After seeing a deer through the window of the train's restaurant car): I hope it doesn't come too close to the train. . .**

YOUNG JULIETA: **It's not afraid of the train. It's looking for a female. It smells her in the air.**

XOAN: **Would you like a drink?**

JULIETA **(Narrating the encounter from the present): Xoan told me his name was Xoan, and I told him mine was Julieta. He told me he was married and that Ana, his wife, had been in a coma for five years. I told him that I was teaching Classical Philology, and that I was substituting for a teacher who was ill. Xoan told me that he was a fisherman, that he had three gamelas. He was going to Madrid to buy an engine for one of them. He also told me that all his life he had lived by the sea, in the house his grandfather bought when he came from Cuba.**

The actors approached the character of Julieta in completely opposite ways. Emma Suárez personified the Julieta wounded by time and circumstances, someone whose emotional armour was cracking under the weight of guilt. To prepare for the role, the actor immersed herself in the work of authors such as Emmanuel Carrère, Marguerite Duras and Michael Cunningham. She studied the paintings of Gerhard Richter, analysed films by Bergman, Malle and Polanski and studied the behaviour of Almodóvar's female characters, in addition to spending many hours in self-imposed solitude. Ugarte, meanwhile, preferred to approach the naivety of the young Julieta from a blank canvas, allowing herself be guided only by the director's instructions. They did not even meet on the set, as Suárez only began filming her scenes once Ugarte had already completed hers. The only time they worked together, at Almodóvar's request, was to rehearse the way they walked so that each one could assimilate and match the other's step.

The result in both cases was a dazzling and delicate performance, brimming with feeling whilst being subtle and concise. The film's contrasts are exemplified by the cinemaphotography of the French Jean-Claude Larrieu which wonderfully merges the muted tones of the night, rain and death, with garments full of bright colours and a predominance of red, present in practically every shot of the film, to emphasise love and blood. Even the settings chosen by Almodóvar evoke different emotions: the Estudio school in Madrid houses the young and dreamy Julieta who begins her work as a teacher, while the Aragonese Pyrenees symbolise the loneliness and helplessness of her older self. The exuberance of the Andalusian estate where the protagonist's parents live reflects the strength of the

ABOVE: Emma Suárez (on the left) prepared for the role by studying *The Year of Magical Thinking* by Joan Didion and *Elevator to the Gallows* by Louis Malle, amongst other works.

family bond, and the Galician coast accompanies the sense of freedom and well-being that envelopes Julieta and Xoan at the beginning of their relationship. 'The landscapes of the film are characters with a dramatic entity,' acknowledged the director, who also had the opportunity to fulfil his long-held wish to shoot on a train – where several reference works of his cinephile repertoire take place, such as *Strangers on a Train* (Alfred Hitchcock, 1951) or *Human Desire* (Fritz Lang, 1954) – and to vindicate its metaphorical power through elements such as snow, isolation and unbridled passion.

Julieta served to reconcile Almodóvar with the critics after the relative disappointment of *I'm So Excited!*, although viewers, especially in Spain, were more sceptical (in France, the film grossed twice as much as in its country of origin, and the reception in Italy was excellent as well). Beyond its repercussions and the different interpretations, what is certain is that Pedro Almodóvar's twentieth feature film was a decisive turning point in his work, a gateway to a much more introspective and serene phase, populated by characters who resurrect the pending accounts of the past and survive in the face of anguish without the balm of humour.

PAIN AND GLORY

BELOW: Antonio Banderas received his first Academy Award nomination for his evocative portrayal of Salvador Mallo.

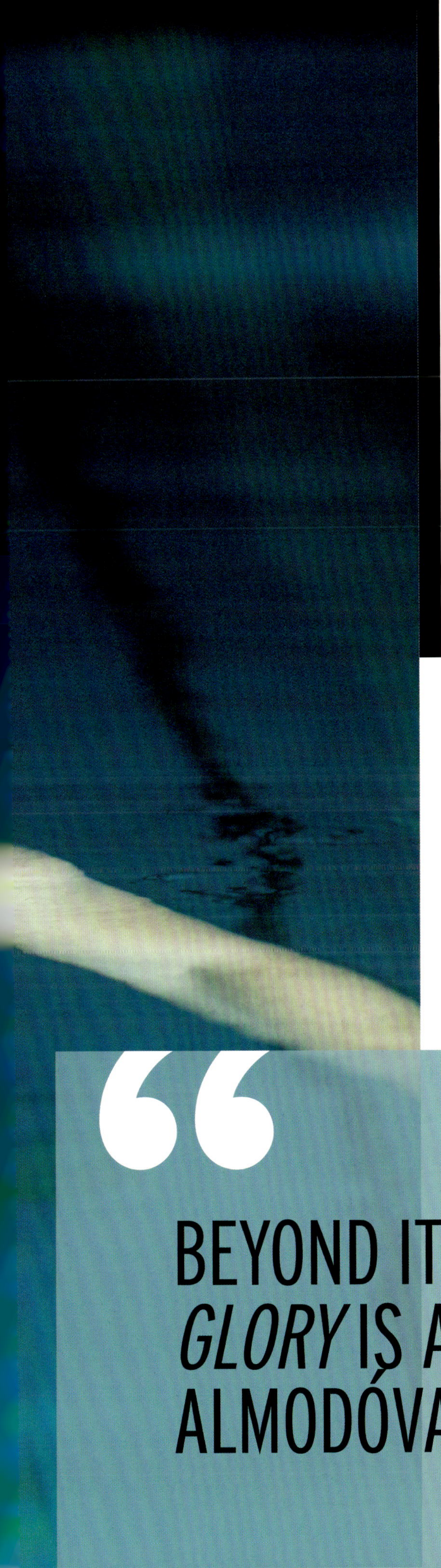

PAIN AND GLORY

Dolor y gloria (2019)

Pain and Glory begins with a man submerged at the bottom of a swimming pool. Salvador Mallo (Antonio Banderas) remains motionless and thoughtful underwater, while we observe the scar that runs along his back as if it were a war wound. Minutes later, a brilliant succession of drawings created by Juan Gatti introduce us to the multiple ailments that afflict the character, who we soon recognise as a successful film director. Among his afflictions, we see tinnitus – an annoying and persistent noise in the ears – powerful migraines and excruciating lower back pain. All conditions that Pedro Almodóvar also suffered from, with a long confinement after back surgery leading him to fear for his ability to continue directing. His therapy in the face of such tremendous pain and debilitating isolation was to write a film that more than any other was inspired by his own experiences: 'The script would not have been possible without knowing the pain that forced me to stay at home. It was born out of that isolation and physical suffering, especially the headaches and back pain. Because once they open you up you are never the same again. . . I didn't want the film to be a whimper, and that's why I resorted to Juan's drawings, a playful way of giving viewers a lot of information and putting them in a situation in a short time.'

Almodóvar has insisted that it is not an autobiographical story, although he acknowledges that he used himself as a model to create his protagonist and those around him. During this period of personal and professional uncertainty, Mallo reunites with an actor

> "BEYOND ITS CHARACTERS, *PAIN AND GLORY* IS A DELICIOUS COMPENDIUM OF ALMODÓVARIAN ELEMENTS."

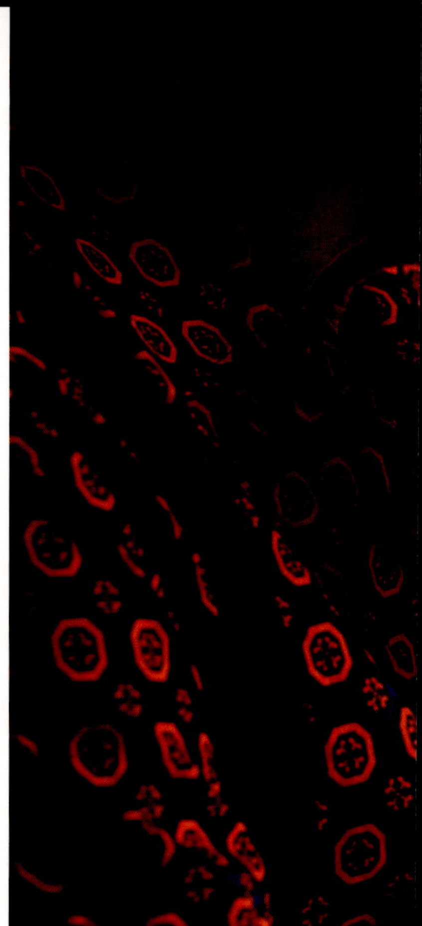

with whom he has had a complicated relationship (Asier Etxeandia), is visited by a former lover (Leonardo Sbaraglia) and receives advice from a compassionate and loyal friend (Nora Navas), all characters based on real figures from the filmmaker's life. And there is, of course, the evocation of the maternal ideal, that cheerful, loving woman, this time played in her youth by Penélope Cruz and in her later years by Julieta Serrano. 'That mother has to do with mine, it's obvious, but on this occasion, I separated myself a little from her by approaching her cinematographically when she gets older. However, there are moments of the character that are taken directly from my own reality, such as when she talks to her son about how he should shroud her when she dies, a moment that comes from the conversations my mother had with my sister on that subject, which they always treated with absolute naturalness.'

Beyond its characters, *Pain and Glory* is a delicious compendium of Almodóvarian elements. Everything, from the filming process seen from the perspective of the creator himself, to the appearance of his own father (representing Mallo's father) in a photomontage with Julieta Serrano, including the mention of Chavela Vargas, the delirious proliferation of taxis or the street where Salvador Mallo lives, all refer to the very intimacy of the director. Production Designer Antxón Gómez oversaw the recreation of the apartment that Almodóvar has in Paseo Rosales in Madrid, down to the very last detail. He built a kitchen almost exactly like the original and adapted the hallway, the lobby and the rest of the spaces to the needs of the production. Even the paintings that Antonio Banderas's character owns – and the odd piece of furniture, such as an armchair or a sideboard – belong to the filmmaker. 'Everything was brought directly from my house, which was very convenient for the production,' he says. 'In fact, I think it was that comfort that made me, for the first time in my career, finish filming ahead of schedule.'

LEFT: Penélope Cruz plays Salvador's mother Jacinta in flashbacks to his childhood in Paterna.

BELOW: Two looks, one direction: Almodóvar shares a moment of meditation with Banderas.

The highest representation of Almodóvar in *Pain and Glory* is found, naturally, in the character of Salvador Mallo. Their hairstyles are almost identical, they are both passionate about tea, and every stitch of the wardrobe worn by Antonio Banderas is an exact replica of the director's own clothes (even the shoes he wears are Almodóvar's own). Despite the personal and artistic relationship that unites them, Banderas was not the first choice for the role. In fact, there was a prolonged casting process with many actors, but none of them convinced the director. In the end, he decided to forget about the search and send the script to Banderas, who accepted the challenge and ended up delivering one of the most brilliant performances of his lengthy career.

'It's the best performance he's ever given in his life,' Almodóvar stated emphatically. 'When we started, Antonio was a passionate animal, who swept everyone away with his mere presence. But now he is different, because he is in maturity and because he has undergone surgery three times [. . .] The Antonio Banderas of today is in a different position: his gestures are very subtle, small. . . And with the film finished, it seems entirely right that it was him who took on my role. Because Antonio is the legitimate protagonist, he is Fellini's Mastroianni in *Eight and a Half*, for many reasons: for having lived hand in hand with me in the eighties, for having worked together, for everything we have done.' The director even told him that, in case of doubt or need, he could imitate him without any problem, but Banderas preferred to create his own portrait of the character, from a very personal perspective. His way of approaching this alter ego comes from wisdom and passion.

Banderas's colossal work is evident in Salvador Mallo's journey through the hells of heroin. The actor gives an overwhelming performance as someone who takes refuge in addiction, only to silence the physical pain of his illnesses and the emotional suffering that comes from not being able to direct the films he writes. During a conversation with his faithful assistant Mercedes, we discover that his desire to forget has even led him to neglect his loved ones, and the character reveals himself to the audience as someone deeply disoriented, lost in the melancholy of his past:

MERCEDES: I'm separating from Luis.

SALVADOR (High on heroin): I didn't know you were having problems.

MERCEDES: I didn't want to bother you. It started a long time ago, and now that I have to spend so much time at home. . . I couldn't keep fooling myself.

SALVADOR: I'm sorry.

MERCEDES: So, if you don't mind, I'd like to keep taking care of your mail. People like to get answers.

SALVADOR: But it's always no. . .

MERCEDES: Well, you should do something. You have too much free time to think about your ailments. Give your brain something to entertain itself, Salvador.

SALVADOR: I'd like to do more things too, Mercedes, but. . .

MERCEDES: You could write. You've got a pile of pages full of ideas you could develop. Shall I make you a list?

SALVADOR: No, I don't want to write if I can't shoot it afterwards. And you know better than anyone that I can't face shooting in these conditions. . . Without shooting, my life has no meaning. But that's the way things are.

ABOVE: Nora Navas, Antonio Banderas and Pedro Almodóvar rehearse the scene in which her character Mercedes shares her marital problems with a heroin-fuelled Salvador.

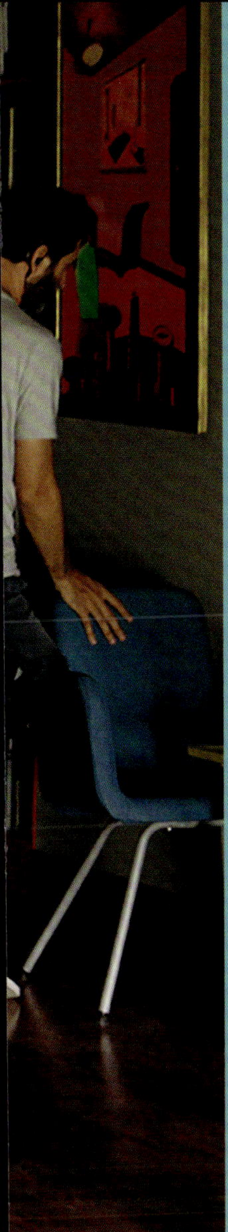

On several occasions, Almodóvar has described the shoot as the most idyllic and happy of his career. The scenes that take place during Mallo's childhood were filmed in the Valencian town of Paterna, in some caves of Moorish origin where, after the Civil War, poor families like his own lived. Most of the scenes were filmed on location, with the interior of one of the caves reproduced in the studio in Madrid. The filmmaker fell in love with this area fifteen years earlier, while he was looking for locations for *Bad Education*, and had always wanted to include them in one of his films because of how much they reminded him of 'the precariousness' with which he grew up in Calzada de Calatrava. Nearby, in Moral de Calatrava, there were houses like those in Paterna, and when at the age of eight he moved with his family to Orellana la Vieja, in Extremadura, he ended up living in a house made of adobe, in a neighbourhood that seemed to him 'out of the Wild West.'

The film had a painless and glory-filled international tour. *Time* magazine chose it as its best movie of 2019, and it was nominated for Best International Feature Film at the Academy Awards, along with a first nomination for the Best Actor Award for Antonio Banderas, though he lost out to Joaquin Phoenix for *Joker* (Todd Phillips, 2019). The reception was so enthusiastic that even Spanish critics, rather circumspect about Almodóvar's most recent works, were ecstatic at such a return to form for the director. *Pain and Glory* emerged as the great winner at the Goya Awards with five wins, including Best Film, Best Director and Best Actor in a Leading Role, and garnered passionate reviews such as that of Luis Martínez in *El Mundo*: 'It reaches a level of perfection that is hard to surpass. The very complicated structure of overlapping times flows without interruption or fissure. Once all the unnecessary elements of folkloric style have been discarded, there remains a sense of purification and clarity very close to the sublime.'

“

IT REACHES A LEVEL OF PERFECTION THAT IS HARD TO SURPASS.

EL MUNDO

”

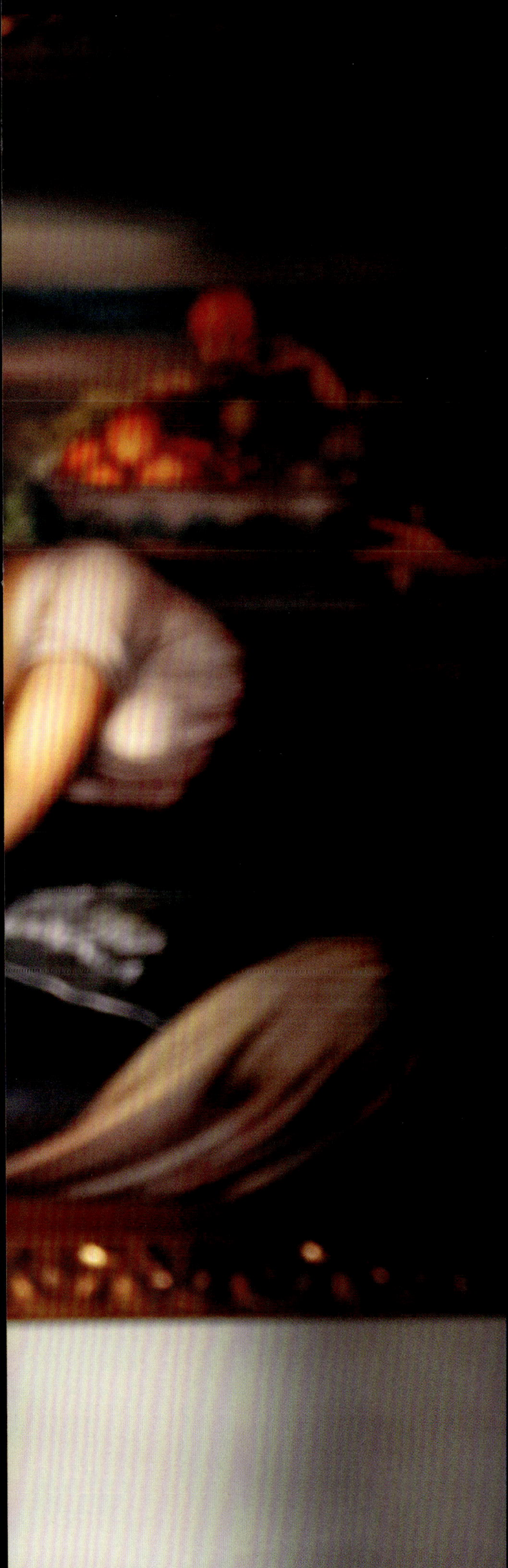

PARALLEL MOTHERS

Profoto

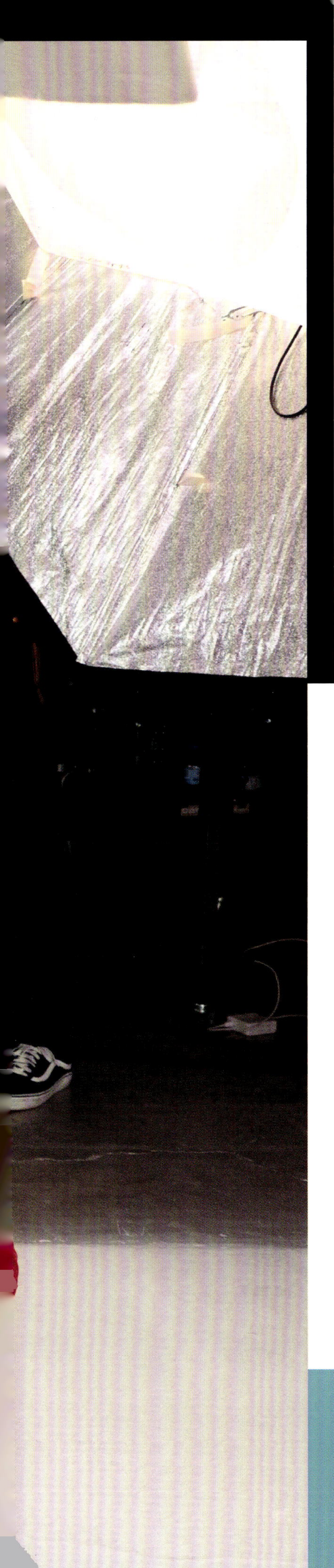

PARALLEL MOTHERS

Madres paralelas (2021)

In March 2020, the Covid-19 pandemic brought the world to a complete standstill. On the 13th, the Spanish government, like others around the world, declared a state of emergency, requiring citizens to confine themselves to their homes due to the unstoppable advance of the disease. Almodóvar was alone in his Madrid apartment, finalising the details for *The Human Voice*, the short film he was about to shoot with Tilda Swinton in early April. The sudden confinement, together with the impossibility of interacting face-to-face with anyone, caused the director great uncertainty and he was so discouraged that he stopped writing for nine days. After that time, he began to capture his thoughts in different articles for the press, in which he narrated how he tried – unsuccessfully – to ignore the growing number of deaths by immersing himself in books, in his memories of Chavela and in James Bond movies. 'If I stop in front of reality, I think I will die. And I don't want to,' he said.

As the days went by, Almodóvar adjusted to the situation, but his mind became progressively more agitated out of sheer boredom. His brother, Agustín, had managed to reschedule the shooting of *The Human Voice* and slowly he found the strength again to develop new ideas, and to revisit some incomplete projects forgotten on his computer. One of these was *Parallel Mothers*, which told the story of the complicity between two single women, of different ages, who meet in a hospital shortly before giving birth. Almodóvar had begun working on the script in the early 2000s, and even visited a maternity ward to investigate the pre-birth ritual and the relationships established between pregnant women. However, some narrative obstacles ended up frustrating his creative impulse and forced him to abandon the story for a period. Until, one day during lockdown, he decided to revisit it. 'When I reviewed it, it seemed different,' he explained. 'Because of the opportunity to concentrate, because no one was going to distract me, I was not going anywhere. I corrected half of the script, and, at that moment, the pieces started to fit.'

Almodóvar found the key to unlocking the plot in an issue that had long troubled him: the murders of men and women during the Spanish Civil War, perpetrated primarily by the Francoist side extrajudicially, or after cursory trials. Many of these victims were buried in mass graves and their families never found their bodies. In recent years, different political

LEFT: Janis, a woman of unbreakable will, who is confronted with a hidden past and unplanned motherhood, is one of the artistic highlights of Penélope Cruz's career.

and legal initiatives in Spain, with the 2007 Historical Memory Law most prominent, had sought restorative judicial measures in favour of those who were persecuted during the conflict and the subsequent dictatorship, although the text exempted the government from the responsibility of exhuming the bodies as stipulated by international law. The issue struck a chord with Almodóvar, who, despite having deliberately ignored the nightmare of Franco's regime in his films, felt a special empathy with those people who struggled to find their disappeared ancestors. 'I felt somehow morally obligated to deal with it. Out of sheer empathy for the relatives of the victims, and because I also believe that this subject would end the Spanish war once and for all. It will remain there until those dead are honoured and that debt is settled.'

The key to unlocking the script was drawing a parallel between motherhood and the search for a missing great-grandfather. Janis (Penélope Cruz), a fashion photographer, becomes pregnant after an affair with a married man, Arturo, a forensic archaeologist, and has invited him to her home village to open a mass grave in which she believes her great-grandfather is buried along with other disappeared villagers. Almodóvar was inspired by a case he had read about of a ten-year-old girl, whose house was taken by three Falangists. Shortly after arriving, they took her father, who was a teacher, to dig his own and other Republican comrades' graves. On the third night, he did not return. 'I chose that little girl to have a very clear memory of the moment when she stopped seeing her father, and I put her in Janis as a grandmother.' Up to that point, the filmmaker had only tackled the dictatorship years in the prologue of *Live Flesh*, also featuring Penélope Cruz and imminent childbirth. With *Parallel Mothers*, he would produce what is undoubtedly his most committed film, focusing as it does on the tragic past of his country.

Almodóvar wrote the character with Penélope Cruz in mind, something he had only done three times in his career: with Carmen Maura in *Women on the Verge of a Nervous Breakdown*, with Antonio Banderas in *Tie Me Up! Tie Me Down!* and with Cruz herself in *Volver*. 'I think it's the most difficult role she's ever played in her life,' confessed the director. 'She has grown hugely as an actress, because she suffers every single thing she does, but establishing enough distance to know that, although she is giving all her soul, it is a recreation, a representation.' Almodóvar rehearsed for months with her and with Milena Smit (who plays Ana, a single teenage mother), a young actor from Alicante who, just two years earlier, was alternating jobs as a waitress, sales clerk, babysitter and information assistant in the subway due to the lack of acting opportunities. Her lucky debut as the femme fatale in *Cross the Line* (*No matarás*, David Victori, 2020) opened wide the doors of the Almodóvarian universe and allowed her to take a very different role, that of a teenager paralysed by uncertainty and fear, a very complex challenge to which she rose admirably. The relationship between the two characters – clear models of the independent and tenacious woman that the director likes so much – is marked by an accidental and traumatic event that takes place shortly after giving birth, while both are still in hospital.

ABOVE: Rossy de Palma (Elena), Israel Elejalde (Arturo), Penélope Cruz and Milena Smit (Ana), in one of the most revealing moments of the film.

“UNDOUBTEDLY HIS MOST COMMITTED FILM, FOCUSING AS IT DOES ON THE TRAGIC PAST OF HIS COUNTRY.”

> SHE HAS GROWN HUGELY AS AN ACTRESS, BECAUSE SHE SUFFERS EVERY SINGLE THING SHE DOES.

ANA: How's your baby?

JANIS: Fine. She's under observation. They only left her with me for a little while. Isn't it wonderful to hear her beating over your heart?

ANA: I can't wait to have her back.

JANIS: Is yours under observation too?

ANA: Yes.

JANIS: Well, that must be normal. . . Mine was born with extrauterine inadaptation, the doctor told me. 'Well, that's a good way to start,' I said. Because that's the life that awaits her, the extrauterine life.

ANA (smiles): Well, yes.

JANIS: But apparently, it's nothing. The poor thing had trouble controlling her breathing outside the womb. What's wrong with yours?

ANA: She seems to have a little low blood sugar. But I've also been told it's nothing.

JANIS: Sure, sure. I'll give you my number if you want to call me.

ANA: OK.

JANIS: Since we're in the same situation, let's talk about it. When do you get the baby?

ANA: Tonight, I think. Or this afternoon.

JANIS: Me too.

RIGHT: If there is one actress who embodies the meaning of motherhood in Almodóvar's work, it is, without a doubt, Penélope Cruz.

When *Parallel Mothers* began filming at the end of March 2021, Spain had recorded more than three million cases of Covid-19 since the beginning of the pandemic, and in Madrid a curfew was still in force every night from 11pm onwards. Making a film in such conditions might have seemed impossible, but the Almodóvar brothers fought fervently to make theirs a reality. They hired nursing staff, conducted thousands of medical tests, and ensured that every member of cast and crew complied with Covid safety restrictions both on and off set.

Production was concentrated in Madrid and its near surroundings, mainly in the town of Torrelaguna, where Janis's emotional journey ends. Two months after the first take, the film completed its principal photography without major complications, in a remarkable display of control and foresight on the part of the professionals at El Deseo. Once the health threat was under control, Almodóvar strove to extract from his story the artistic excellence that characterises his work: exquisite performances (we must not forget the work of Aitana Sánchez-Gijón and Israel Elejalde), warmth and formal splendour, and a beautifully poetic reference to Federico García Lorca and the unhealed wounds of Spain's fascist past.

The post-production process was one of the fastest in the director's filmography. With its premiere set for early October, *Parallel Mothers* arrived in time to be screened at the Mostra di Venezia with overwhelming success, winning a well-deserved Volpi Cup for Best Actress for Penélope Cruz. The film also received several nominations at the Golden Globe, BAFTA and European Film awards, garnering some of the most glowing reviews of Almodóvar's career and topping the French box office in its first weekend, the director's best result in the country since *Volver*. Nor did the Oscars forget the film, awarding it nominations for Best Original Score – Alberto Iglesias here completes a prodigious composition, always linked to the inner world of the protagonist – and for Best Actress, the fourth for Cruz in her career.

ABOVE: Israel Elejalde as Arturo, a forensic anthropologist who will end up playing a decisive role in Janis's life.

LEFT: The film was shot during the spring of 2021, in the midst of heavy security measures due to the Covid-19 pandemic.

EPILOGUE

EPILOGUE

An Artist for the World

We have already seen how, for decades, Pedro Almodóvar was able to resist the temptation of Anglo-Saxon cinema and the big Hollywood stars. Although he was widely recognised by the industry and received a multitude of stimulating proposals, he always remained faithful to the Spanish idiosyncrasy of his stories. However, after *Pain and Glory*, something changed. In a way, that exercise of personal and professional atonement represented the culmination of a dazzling introspective period, a settling of accounts where the roots and traces of the past formed an indissoluble part of the characters' souls. After that film, Almodóvar felt ready to explore the unknown and adapt his artistic personality to the universal language of cinema. He had been hesitating for some time about whether or not to take the plunge into shooting in English, with an international cast and a much deeper thematic and geographic scope. 'I wanted to experience how I moved within the language, how I saw myself directing in English,' he said, 'although I preferred to do it as a short, because in a long film I didn't dare.' The decision was made: Almodóvar would shoot for the first time in a foreign language, and he would do it through an old acquaintance – the short film – as a dress rehearsal to tackle a longer story in the future. In the end, due to the pandemic (or thanks to it), he still had time to approach for one last time the history and context of his country with the wonderful and overwhelming *Parallel Mothers*.

RIGHT: In *The Human Voice*, Tilda Swinton became the first actress with whom Almodóvar filmed entirely in English.

"I WANTED TO EXPERIENCE HOW I MOVED WITHIN THE LANGUAGE, HOW I SAW MYSELF DIRECTING IN ENGLISH."

N°5
CHANEL

The chosen text was also particularly familiar to him. It is worth remembering that *The Human Voice*, the 1930 monologue by Jean Cocteau, written for the greater glory of Edith Piaf, was one of Almodóvar's favourite pieces and an essential reference point in his films, present in titles such as *Law of Desire*, *The Flower of My Secret* and, above all, *Women on the Verge of a Nervous Breakdown*. Faced with the experience of working in English, the director needed a terrain on which to move with total confidence, and this story about a woman abandoned by her lover, which he had so often analysed and reinterpreted, was perfect for it. 'It proposes a female character in a situation that I like very much or, at least, in which I manage very well as a writer. The grieving woman is a subject that I find very inspiring,' he acknowledged. 'However, when faced with the original text, I realised that I did not identify with that woman. With the pain, yes, but not with that part of submission. I made her more mine, more contemporary, more in control of herself.' To play her, Almodóvar turned to Tilda Swinton, one of the most fascinating actors of recent times, Oscar winner for *Michael Clayton* (Tony Gilroy, 2007) and muse of such sublime filmmakers as Jim Jarmusch, Wes Anderson and the Coen brothers.

The Human Voice condenses in twenty-eight minutes the entire essence of its director's tragic tale: a woman who is a victim of despair, self-imposed solitude as a way of escape, baroque colours, homicidal impulse, sudden rebellion against the harmful man. Swinton amazingly composes a character on the edge of her own destruction, wounded and misguided, who finds the only way to freedom is through revenge. Almodóvar also surrounds

> THIS IS A QUEER WESTERN, IN THE SENSE THAT THERE ARE TWO MEN, AND THEY LOVE EACH OTHER.

LEFT: Almodóvar was able to subvert the rules of the western – a genre that always appealed to him as a viewer – in his masterful short film *Strange Way of Life*.

himself with his trusted artistic circle (José Luis Alcaine in photography, Teresa Font in editing, Alberto Iglesias in composition) and offers one of his most vigorous and melodramatic works, where even the sobriety of this new language is imbued with unbridled passion, with that suggested and invisible blood, and even with a purifying fire.

Filming took place over twelve days in July 2020, amid strict security measures due to the Covid-19 pandemic. A little over a month later, on 3 September, *The Human Voice* was screened at the Mostra di Venezia to the delight of a devoted public, despite the restrictions and extreme control of seating capacity. Precisely in this very Kafkaesque context for theatres, Almodóvar was able to release the film at the end of October of that cursed year. While the big studios were cancelling one after another their main bets for the big screen, he achieved the unusual feat of programming a short film in more than a hundred Spanish cinemas and made it the highest grossing in the history of the country.

In early 2022, three months after the premiere of *Parallel Mothers*, the long-awaited announcement arrived: Almodóvar would shoot his first film in English, adapting five of the forty-three stories that make up *A Manual for Cleaning Women*, a sensational anthology in which writer Lucia Berlin turned her own experiences – full of humour and emotion – into a survival notebook for women from around the world. Leading the cast, and as producer, would be two-time Oscar winner Cate Blanchett. 'I'm so excited that we finally get to make it,' the Australian actor declared shortly after the news broke. 'No one can create roles as moving as Pedro. . . Women talking to women about surreal things that on the surface are bizarre, but at the same time are very realistic.' However, nine months later Almodóvar unexpectedly announced his departure from the project: 'It has been a very painful decision for me. I have dreamed of working with Cate for a long time. But unfortunately, I no longer feel capable of making this film in its entirety.'

Among the reasons that led to his withdrawal, the director acknowledged that he did not feel physically prepared for a shoot that would take place in several countries, and also that he was going to need a time for rehearsals that a cast of this calibre, so much in demand with different projects around the world, could not guarantee. 'The problem would be me with my back and so many locations. And I would also have problems with the actors, who were all stars. There were a lot of new things: everything was period, and everything was on a set, and everything was made in a factory. I'm very obsessive about that. . . Everything that appears in my films has passed through my hands and has been selected from a lot of options,' he confessed months after the cancellation of the film, which he had intended to shoot mainly in Alicante's Ciudad de la Luz. 'It was scheduled to start in January 2022, but Cate told me that I had to wait because she had projects throughout the year. So I sat on my hands and had a whole year to think about it.'

The disappointment of his failed project with Cate Blanchett did not prevent Almodóvar from continuing with the plan initiated with *The Human Voice*. In fact, the filmmaker's next step in this process of idiomatic and narrative adaptation was going to be a challenge of imposing proportions: nothing less than a western, undoubtedly the quintessential North American genre and a cinematographic model in complete opposition to his films, always so intimate and geographically defined. Almodóvar wrote the script for *Strange Way of Life* during lockdown, just after completing that of *Parallel Mothers*, and conceived the story as a medium-length film that would completely reverse the idea of masculinity in western films, always linked to a heterosexual and conservative context. 'My cowboys say things that have never been heard in this genre. . . This is a queer western, in the sense that there are two men, and they love each other, but they live that situation in opposite ways,' the director pointed out, in reference to the protagonists, two former hired gunslingers who meet again twenty-five years after seeing each other for the last time. One works as a rancher and the other as a sheriff in the town of Bitter Creek. However, beneath this old friendship hides a feeling that time has not been able to attenuate, and that will once again come between the two characters and their respective passions.

Strange Way of Life owes its title to the famous fado by singer Amália Rodrigues, whose lyrics suggest that there is no stranger existence than that which is lived with one's back to one's own desire (the song can be heard at the beginning of the film in a version by Caetano Veloso). Almodóvar completed filming in August 2022 in the desert of Tabernas, in Almería – specifically in the cowboy village built by Sergio Leone in the 1960s to shoot his legendary *Dollars Trilogy* with Clint Eastwood, and which Almodóvar found 'full of rust and dust that had eaten the sets but made them look less artificial' – with a cast headed by the undisputed icon of indie cinema Ethan Hawke and Pedro Pascal, star of TV series *Narcos*, *The Mandalorian* and

“HIS STORIES ARE UNIVERSAL BECAUSE THEY SPEAK OF EMOTIONS, OF PEOPLE WHO SUFFER AND LOVE.”

The Last of Us. Despite the peculiarity of the genre, the filmmaker was able to convey not only the plot premise but also the aesthetic line of his films, and decided to call on Anthony Vaccarello, creative director of Saint Laurent, for the costume design and the accessories that appear on the screen.

Strange Way of Life, like *The Human Voice* before it, was the necessary preparation to the inevitable. In the early months of 2024, Almodóvar began filming his first English-language feature, *The Room Next Door*, between New York and Madrid and starring Tilda Swinton and Julianne Moore. The plot revolves around the relationship between a war reporter and an autofiction novelist, and the progressive emotional bond they establish as writers. A situation that the author himself defines as "extreme and strangely sweet", and which stands as the central axis of a film that also speaks about "the limitless cruelty of wars, death, friendship and sexual pleasure as the best allies in the fight against horror". *The Room Next Door* is the definitive demonstration that Pedro Almodóvar's art is not limited to a specific area and audience but can be experienced from multiple perspectives.

Almodóvar's stories do not belong to anyone. They move without distinction. They do not understand ideologies, gender, race or borders. They are not even his own, because, once shared, they accompany us forever.

They belong to the world.

BELOW: The director poses with one of his cowboys, Pedro Pascal (Silva).

ABOVE: Cecilia Roth's natural magnetism and beauty made her the perfect choice for the lead role in *Labyrinth of Passion*.

AFTERWORD

When I think about how I met Pedro, memories come flooding back. Actually, I have several perspectives regarding that meeting.

The first has to do with some friends in common, starting with Gustavo Pérez de Ayala. I was eighteen or nineteen, and one fine day Gustavo told me that, every Friday, a friend of his organised a meal at a trendy restaurant in Madrid. I was invited to one and there I was introduced to Pedro, who seemed as lost as me. I was immediately attracted by his humour, his grace, and his very relaxed attitude. It was not something that was common in Spain at that time.

The second memory takes me to the San Sebastián Festival in 1977. Although I was still very young, that year there were two of my films in the official section: *De fresa, limón y menta*, directed by Miguel Ángel Díez, and another Argentinian film entitled *No toquen a la nena*, by Juan José Jusid. At that time, all the films were screened at the Maria Cristina, next to the Reina Victoria, the hotel where we stayed. On the same street, on the corner, there was a tapas bar where absolutely everyone went. That was where they did the interviews, always with lots of curious people around. Among all of them, my attention was always drawn to Pedro, who was extremely enthusiastic about film and never missed a single edition of the festival.

And there is still a third way to explain how we met. Shortly after arriving in Spain, I got close to a group of people in an almost natural way, for purely temporal and geographical reasons. I mean people like Iván Zulueta, Eusebio Poncela, Will More, Marta Fernández-Muro, Laura García Lorca... And Pedro, of course. I was the youngest, and for me they were my teachers of cinema, literature and life.

Pepi, Luci, Bom was like a game for me. The camera was Pedro's, and Pepón Coromina, I think his first producer, believed in his talent. The script was marvellous, very daring for that time in Spain. Finding something like this was totally unusual... There was an advertisement for 'Bragas Ponte,' which served all kinds of feminine needs. Over time, that phrase has become a kind of advice to never forget what is essential. *'Hagas lo que hagas, Ponte bragas'* ('Whatever you do, put on panties').

I was very amused by everything Pedro invented about my participation in the film. I had a lot of fun. We shot on weekends because Pedro was loyal to Telefónica during the week. I think that, for that reason, I was never too conscious of making a film. For me it was like filming a piece of life, like when your parents film you blowing out your birthday candles. And in relation to Pedro, I knew I would do anything he could ask of me. He trusted me more than I trusted myself.

Labyrinth of Passion was another movie so irreverent that I find it hard to believe it could be filmed in present-day Spain. I doubt very much that his way of making humour, of interpreting reality, could be understood today as irony. Pedro was ahead of his time, for what he told, for the characters he invented (which we eventually saw in real life... ahead of time), and because of him I had a great time filming again. However, now I was aware of being inside a movie. When I saw it again after almost thirty years, I discovered extraordinary and unthinkable characters for the time, such as the psychologist or the doctor played by Fernando Vivanco. That is something that Pedro has always had: he can see something possible in the smoke, for in his head there is no situation that cannot happen. The coincidences in his films are so plausible that although in real life they would be improbable, in his films they take on the certainty that needs a truth to settle in, and you believe that the son of the Emperor of Tiran lives in Madrid (which is the most modern city in the world) during his exile, and that there he meets exactly who he needs to meet.

Then came small appearances in *Dark Habits* and *What Have I Done to Deserve This?*, until in 1986 I returned to Buenos Aires. I planned to stay only twenty days (I had to return to Spain to shoot *Lulú de noche* with Emilio Martínez-Lázaro), but I decided to stay indefinitely because I felt that, at that moment, that was my place.

During all the time I spent in Argentina, I distanced myself from Spanish cinema. Despite this, I never stopped thinking about working with Pedro again. I went to Madrid two or three times a year to see my friends, and even shot a series or a film from time to time. Until *Martín* (*Hache*) arrived, and I imagine that Pedro wanted us to shoot together again. We were very close when the film was released. In fact, I remember perfectly when we were doing our make-up together with Bibi in a room at the Palace Hotel. That night I won the Goya and a new panorama opened up for me in Spanish cinema. Months later, it was summer in Argentina and the phone started ringing. It was the unmistakable voice of Pedro, who told me that he was preparing a film about women, and that he wanted me to play the main character. I remember hanging up and in seconds going through all kinds of emotions possible in such a short time: I was laughing, jumping, screaming, crying. . . I was in a state of adrenalin-fuelled excitement. I would never have imagined that he would call me right then and there, that he would call me for a film like *All About My Mother*, and that he would then go through everything we went through with it. When he sent me the script, I connected at once and understood Manuela, her journey, that wonderful empathy between female characters. The help that these women give each other is so moving, so brutal, that it alleviates what is impossible to alleviate, which is the death of a child. Pedro manages to keep the character in a very particular state, flooded with all the love she has been able to receive. Instead of becoming resentful, Manuela understands that life is suffering, also love and stumbles, but never evil. The possibility of a generous life, despite the pain of losing her son, still seems to me something very complex from a rational point of view.

After Manuela came other characters of Pedro's that I adore, like the ones he entrusted to me in films such as *I'm So Excited!* and *Pain and Glory*, although neither he nor I are the same as we were in those early years. Everything we did then was full of joy and future, and the idea that it might end at some point never crossed our minds. However, the things that happen to us now are different, and I think that Pedro has had the enormous courage to always shoot what he needs to tell at that moment. . . And not only in that: he has also been brave, as always, making decisions within each of his films.

I feel very close to his sensitivity, and I know that we can share similar views on many things. I still have a deep feeling of enormous affection for and curiosity about him, and I consider him to have been one of the people who have most influenced me in many aspects of my life. Because there are people who, for some reason, can touch deep fibres of your biology, of your organism.

Pedro Almodóvar is one of them.

Cecilia Roth

TOP: Almodóvar, during the filming of *Julieta*.

ABOVE: The filmmaker with Cecilia Roth and Rosa Maria Sardà on the set of *All About My Mother*.

RIGHT: Reunited on *I'm So Excited!* fourteen years after the film that led them to Oscar glory.

FILMOGRAPHY

FEATURE FILMS

PEPI, LUCI, BOM AND OTHER GIRLS LIKE MOM
(Pepi, Luci, Bom y otras chicas del montón)
(Fígaro Films)
80 minutes
Writer: Pedro Almodóvar
Director of Photography: Paco Femenía
Cast: Carmen Maura (Pepi), Félix Rotaeta (The Policeman), Alaska (Bom), Eva Siva (Luci).
Release Date: 27 October 1980

LABYRINTH OF PASSION
(Laberinto de pasiones)
(Musidora / Alphaville)
100 minutes
Writer: Pedro Almodóvar
Director of Photography: Ángel Luis Fernández
Cast: Cecilia Roth (Sexilia), Imanol Arias (Riza Niro), Helga Liné (Toraya), Marta Fernández-Muro (Queti), Fernando Vivanco (Doctor), Antonio Banderas (Sadec).
Release Date: 7 September 1982

DARK HABITS
(Entre tinieblas)
(Tesauro)
110 minutes
Writer: Pedro Almodóvar
Director of Photography: Ángel Luis Fernández
Cast: Cristina S. Pascual (Yolanda Bel), Julieta Serrano (Mother Superior), Marisa Paredes (Sister Manure), Mari Carrillo (Marchioness), Lina Canalejas (Sister Snake), Manuel Zarzo (Chaplain), Carmen Maura (Sister Damned), Chus Lampreave (Sister Rat).
Release Date: 3 October 1983

WHAT HAVE I DONE TO DESERVE THIS?
(¿Qué he hecho yo para merecer esto!!)
(Tesauro / Kaktus Producciones Cinematográficas)
100 minutes
Writer: Pedro Almodóvar
Director of Photography: Ángel Luis Fernández
Cast: Carmen Maura (Gloria), Luis Hostalot (Polo), Gonzalo Suárez (Lucas Villalba), Ángel de Andrés López (Antonio), Verónica Forqué (Crystal), Kiti Manver (Juani), Chus Lampreave (Grandmother), Juan Martínez (Toni), Emilio Gutiérrez Caba (Pedro), Amparo Soler Leal (Patricia).
Release Date: 25 October 1984

MATADOR
(Compañía Iberoamericana de TV / Televisión Española)
110 minutes
Writer: Pedro Almodóvar
Director of Photography: Ángel Luis Fernández
Cast: Assumpta Serna (María Cardenal), Nacho Martínez (Diego), Antonio Banderas (Ángel), Eva Cobo (Eva), Julieta Serrano (Berta), Chus Lampreave (Pilar), Carmen Maura (Julia), Eusebio Poncela (Superintendent Del Valle).
Release Date: 7 March 1986

THE LAW OF DESIRE
(La ley del deseo)
(El Deseo / Lauren Films)
102 minutes
Writer: Pedro Almodóvar
Director of Photography: Ángel Luis Fernández
Cast: Eusebio Poncela (Pablo Quintero), Carmen Maura (Tina Quintero), Antonio Banderas (Antonio Benítez), Miguel Molina (Juan Bermúdez), Fernando Guillén (Police Inspector), Manuela Velasco (Ada).
Release Date: 7 February 1987

WOMEN ON THE VERGE OF A NERVOUS BREAKDOWN
(Mujeres al borde de un ataque de nervios)
(El Deseo / Lauren Films)
88 minutes
Writer: Pedro Almodóvar
Director of Photography: José Luis Alcaine
Cast: Carmen Maura (Pepa), Antonio Banderas (Carlos), Julieta Serrano (Lucía), María Barranco (Candela), Rossy de Palma (Marisa), Guillermo Montesinos (Taxi Driver), Kiti Manver (Paulina Morales), Chus Lampreave (The Concierge), Loles León (Cristina), Fernando Guillén (Iván).
Release Date: 23 March 1988

TIE ME UP! TIE ME DOWN!
(¡Átame!)
(El Deseo)
111 minutes
Writer: Pedro Almodóvar
Director of Photography: José Luis Alcaine
Cast: Victoria Abril (Marina Osorio), Antonio Banderas (Ricki), Loles León (Lola), Julieta Serrano (Alma), María Barranco (Doctor), Francisco Rabal (Máximo Espejo), Rossy de Palma (Woman on Vespa).
Release Date: 22 January 1990

HIGH HEELS
(Tacones lejanos)
(El Deseo / TF1)
113 minutes
Writer: Pedro Almodóvar
Director of Photography: Alfredo Mayo
Cast: Victoria Abril (Rebeca), Marisa Paredes (Becky del Páramo), Miguel Bosé (Judge Domínguez), Ana Lizarán (Margarita), Cristina Marcos (Paula), Féodor Atkine (Manuel).
Release Date: 23 October 1991

KIKA
(El Deseo / TF1)
114 minutes
Writer: Pedro Almodóvar
Director of Photography: Alfredo Mayo
Cast: Verónica Forqué (Kika), Peter Coyote (Nicholas Pierce), Victoria Abril (Andrea Caracortada), Álex Casanovas (Ramón), Rossy de Palma (Juana), Santiago Lajusticia (Paul Bazzo), Anabel Alonso (Amparo), Bibiana Fernández (Susana).
Release Date: 25 October 1993

THE FLOWER OF MY SECRET
(La flor de mi secreto)
(El Deseo / TF1)
103 minutes
Writer: Pedro Almodóvar
Director of Photography: Affonso Beato
Cast: Marisa Paredes (Leo Macías), Juan Echanove (Ángel), Carmen Elías (Betty), Rossy de Palma (Rosa), Chus Lampreave (Mother), Imanol Arias (Paco), Joaquín Cortés (Antonio), Manuela Vargas (Blanca).
Release Date: 20 September 1995

LIVE FLESH
(Carne trémula)
(El Deseo / France 3 Cinéma)
100 minutes
Writers: Pedro Almodóvar, Jorge Guerricaechevarría and Ray Loriga, based on the novel by Ruth Rendell
Director of Photography: Affonso Beato
Cast: Javier Bardem (David), Francesca Neri (Elena), Liberto Rabal (Víctor), Ángela Molina (Clara), José Sancho (Sancho), Penélope Cruz (Isabel), Pilar Bardem (Miss Centro de Mesa).
Release Date: 9 October 1997

ALL ABOUT MY MOTHER
(Todo sobre mi madre)
(El Deseo / Renn Productions / France 2 Cinéma)
101 minutes
Writer: Pedro Almodóvar
Director of Photography: Affonso Beato
Cast: Cecilia Roth (Manuela), Marisa Paredes (Huma Rojo), Antonia San Juan (Agrado), Penélope Cruz (Rosa), Candela Peña (Nina), Rosa María Sardà (Rosa's Mother), Fernando Fernán Gómez (Rosa's Father), Toni Cantó (Lola), Eloy Azorín (Esteban).
Release Date: 16 April 1999

TALK TO HER
(Hable con ella)
(El Deseo)
109 minutes
Writer: Pedro Almodóvar
Director of Photography: Javier Aguirresarobe
Cast: Javier Cámara (Benigno Martín), Darío Grandinetti (Marco Zuluaga), Leonor Watling (Alicia), Rosario Flores (Lydia González), Mariola Fuentes (Rosa), Geraldine Chaplin (Katerina Bilova), Paz Vega (Amparo), Fele Martínez (Alfredo).
Release Date: 15 March 2002

BAD EDUCATION
(La mala educación)
(El Deseo)
109 minutes
Writer: Pedro Almodóvar
Director of Photography: José Luis Alcaine
Cast: Gael García Bernal (Ángel / Juan / Zahara), Fele Martínez (Enrique Goded), Daniel Giménez Cacho (Father Manuel), Lluís Homar (Manuel Berenguer), Javier Cámara (Paquito), Francisco Maestre (Father José), Francisco Boira (Ignacio).
Release Date: 19 March 2004

VOLVER
(El Deseo)
110 minutes
Writer: Pedro Almodóvar
Director of Photography: José Luis Alcaine
Cast: Penélope Cruz (Raimunda), Carmen Maura (Irene), Lola Dueñas (Sole), Blanca Portillo (Agustina), Yohana Cobo (Paula), Chus Lampreave (Aunt Paula), Antonio de la Torre (Paco).
Release Date: 16 March 2006

BROKEN EMBRACES
(Los abrazos rotos)
(El Deseo)
125 minutes
Writer: Pedro Almodóvar
Director of Photography: Rodrigo Prieto

Cast: Penélope Cruz (Lena), Lluís Homar (Mateo Blanco / Harry Caine), Blanca Portillo (Judit García), José Luis Gómez (Ernesto Martel), Rubén Ochandiano (Ernesto Martel Jr. / Ray X), Tamar Novas (Diego), Ángela Molina (Lena's Mother).
Release Date: 18 March 2009

THE SKIN I LIVE IN
(La piel que habito)
(El Deseo)
118 minutes
Writer: Pedro Almodóvar, based on the novel *Tarantula* by Thierry Jonquet
Director of Photography: José Luis Alcaine
Cast: Antonio Banderas (Dr. Robert Ledgard), Elena Anaya (Vera), Marisa Paredes (Marilia), Jan Cornet (Vicente), Roberto Álamo (Zeca), Eduard Fernández (Fulgencio), Blanca Suárez (Norma), Bárbara Lennie (Cristina).
Release Date: 2 September 2011

I'M SO EXCITED!
(Los amantes pasajeros)
(El Deseo)
90 minutes
Writer: Pedro Almodóvar
Director of Photography: José Luis Alcaine
Cast: Antonio de la Torre (Álex Acero), Hugo Silva (Benito Morón), Javier Cámara (Joserra), Carlos Areces (Fajas), Raúl Arévalo (Ulloa), José María Yazpik (Infante), Cecilia Roth (Norma Boss), Lola Dueñas (Bruna), Guillermo Toledo (Ricardo Galán), José Luis Torrijo (Sr. Más), Miguel Ángel Silvestre (Groom), Laya Martí (Bride), Paz Vega (Alba), Blanca Suárez (Ruth), Antonio Banderas (León), Penélope Cruz (Jessica).
Release Date: 8 March 2013

JULIETA
(El Deseo)
96 minutes
Writer: Pedro Almodóvar, based on the short stories "Chance", "Soon" and "Silence" by Alice Munro
Director of Photography: Jean-Claude Larrieu
Cast: Emma Suárez (Julieta), Adriana Ugarte (Young Julieta), Daniel Grao (Xoan), Inma Cuesta (Ava), Darío Grandinetti (Lorenzo), Michelle Jenner (Beatriz), Pilar Castro (Claudia), Nathalie Poza (Juana), Susi Sánchez (Sara).
Release Date: 8 April 2016

PAIN AND GLORY
(Dolor y gloria)
(El Deseo)
113 minutes
Writer: Pedro Almodóvar
Director of Photography: José Luis Alcaine
Cast: Antonio Banderas (Salvador Mallo), Asier Etxeandia (Alberto Crespo), Leonardo Sbaraglia (Federico Delgado), Nora Navas (Mercedes), Julieta Serrano (Jacinta), Penélope Cruz (Young Jacinta), César Vicente (Eduardo), Asier Flores (Young Salvador), Cecilia Roth (Zulema), Raúl Arévalo (Venancio Mallo).
Release Date: 22 March 2019

PARALLEL MOTHERS
(Madres paralelas)
(El Deseo)
123 minutes
Writer: Pedro Almodóvar
Director of Photography: José Luis Alcaine
Cast: Penélope Cruz (Janis), Milena Smit (Ana), Israel Elejalde (Arturo), Aitana Sánchez-Gijón (Teresa), Rossy de Palma (Elena), Julieta Serrano (Brígida).
Release Date: 8 October 2021

AMATEUR & SHORT FILMS

Film político
4 minutes
Writer: Pedro Almodóvar
1974

Dos putas, o historia de amor que termina en boda
10 minutes
Writer: Pedro Almodóvar
1974

Blancor
5 minutes
Writer: Pedro Almodóvar
1975

La caída de Sodoma
10 minutes
Writer: Pedro Almodóvar
1975

Homenaje
10 minutes
Writer: Pedro Almodóvar
1975

El sueño, o la estrella
12 minutes
Writer: Pedro Almodóvar
1975

Muerte en la carretera
(Ajax Films)
8 minutes
Writer: Pedro Almodóvar
Director of Photography: Roberto Gómez
Cast: Paloma Hurtado, Juan Lombardero, Pepe Maya, Miguel Ángel Requejo.
1976

Sea caritativo
5 minutes
Writer: Pedro Almodóvar
1976

Tráiler de Who's Afraid of Virginia Woolf?
5 minutes
Writer: Pedro Almodóvar
1976

Sexo va, sexo viene
17 minutes
Writer: Pedro Almodóvar
1977

Las tres ventajas de Ponte
5 minutes
Writer: Pedro Almodóvar
1977

Complementos
10 minutes
Writer: Pedro Almodóvar
1977

Salomé
(Manuela Films)
12 minutes
Writer: Pedro Almodóvar, based on the play by Oscar Wilde
Director of Photography: Luciano Berriatúa
Cast: Isabel Mestres (Salomé), Fernando Hilbeck (Abraham), Agustín Almodóvar (Isaac), Juan Lombardero (Voice of God).
1978

Folle... Folle... Fólleme Tim!
90 minutes
Writer: Pedro Almodóvar
Cast: Eva Siva, Carmen Maura, Kiti Mánver, Pedro Almodóvar.
1978

Tráiler para amantes de lo prohibido
(RTVE)
17 minutes
Writer: Pedro Almodóvar
Cast: Josele Román (Wife), Bibiana Fernández (Lili Put), Sonia Hoffman (Daughter), Pau Poch (Husband).
1985

Pastas Ardilla
1 minute
Writer: Pedro Almodóvar
Cast: Rossy de Palma, Chus Lampreave.
1996

THE CANNIBALISTIC COUNCILLOR
(La concejala antropófaga)
(El Deseo)
8 minutes
Writer: Pedro Almodóvar (as Harry "Huracán" Caine)
Director of Photography: Joaquín Manchado
Cast: Carmen Machi (Chon), Penélope Cruz (Pina), Marta Aledo (Maribel).
2009

THE HUMAN VOICE
(La voz humana)
(El Deseo)
28 minutes
Writer: Pedro Almodóvar, based on the play *La voix humaine*, by Jean Cocteau
Director of Photography: José Luis Alcaine
Cast: Tilda Swinton, Agustín Almodóvar, Miguel Almodóvar, Pablo Almodóvar.
2020

STRANGE WAY OF LIFE
(Extraña forma de vida)
31 minutes
Writer: Pedro Almodóvar
Director of Photography: José Luis Alcaine
Cast: Pedro Pascal (Silva), Ethan Hawke (Jake), Manu Ríos (Singer), Jason Fernández (Young Jake), Pedro Casablanc (Carpenter), Sara Sálamo (Conchita), José Condessa (Young Silva).
2023

MUSIC DEPARTMENT

Labyrinth of Passion (Writer / Performer)
'Suck It to Me', 'Gran Ganga'

Dark Habits (Writer / Performer)
'Suck It to Me'

The Law of Desire (Writer / Performer)
'Voy a ser mama', 'Susan Get Down', 'Satanasa'

Tie Me Up! Tie Me Down! (Writer /

Performer)
'Satanasa'

High Heels (Lyrics)
'Un año de amor'

The L Word (TV Series)
(Anonymous Content / Dufferin Gate Productions / Showtime Networks / Viacom Production)
Episode *L'Ennui* (Lyrics)
'Un año de amor'
2004

Bad Education (Soundtrack)
'Torna a Surriento'

El Calentito
(Vértice 360 / Estudios Picasso / Canal+ España)
90 minutes
Director: Chus Gutiérrez
Writers: Chus Gutiérrez, Juan Carlos Rubio
Director of Photography: Kiko de la Rica
Songs: 'Suck It to Me' (Perfomer / Writer)
Cast: Verónica Sánchez, Macarena Gómez, Juan Sanz.
2005

Cuéntame cómo pasó (TV Series)
(Grupo Ganga Producciones / TVE)
Episode *La movida y mucho más* (Performer / Writer)
'Suck It to Me'
2013

El Ministerio del Tiempo (TV Series)
(Cliffhanger / Netflix / Onza Partners)
Episode *El laberinto del tiempo* (Performer / Writer)
'Suck It to Me'
2020

ACTOR

Film político (Self)

A Man Called Autumn Flower
(Un hombre llamado Flor de Otoño)
(José Frade Producciones Cinematográficas / Panorámica)
100 minutes
Director: Pedro Olea
Writers: Pedro Olea, Rafael Azcona
Director of Photography: Fernando Arribas
Cast: José Sacristán, Francisco Algora, Carmen Carbonell, Roberto Camardiel, Carlos Piñeiro, Pedro Almodóvar (Lola Nicaragua).
1978

Times of the Constitution
(Tiempos de Constitución)
(Rafael Gordon Producciones)
101 minutes
Director: Rafael Gordon
Writer: Rafael Gordon
Director of Photography: Miguel Ángel Martín Sánchez
Cast: Francisco Algora, Verónica Forqué, Héctor Alterio, José Bódalo, Kiti Mánver, Alfonso del Real, Pedro Almodóvar.
1978

What's a Girl Like You Doing in a Place Like This?
(¿Qué hace una chica como tú en un sitio como este?)
(La Salamandra Producciones Cinematográficas)
85 minutes
Director: Fernando Colomo
Writers: Fernando Colomo, Jaime Chávarri
Director of Photography: Javier Aguirresarobe
Cast: Carmen Maura, Félix Rotaeta, Héctor Alterio, José Lage, Pedro Beltrán, Tony Canal, Marta Fernández Muro, Mercedes Sampietro, Pedro Almodóvar (Spectator).
1978

Folle... Folle... Fólleme Tim! (Man)

Rapture
(Arrebato)
(Nicolás Astiarraga P.C.)
Director: Iván Zulueta
Writer: Iván Zulueta
Director of Photography: Ángel Luis Fernández
Cast: Eusebio Poncela, Cecilia Roth, Will More, Marta Fernández Muro, Helena Fernán-Gómez, Carmen Giralt, Pedro Almodóvar (Gloria's Voice).
1979

Pepi, Luci, Bom & Other Girls Like Mom (Master of Ceremonies)

Labyrinth of Passion (Singer and Photo Novel Director)

Dark Habits (Bus Passenger)

What Have I Done to Deserve This? (Singer)

La bola de cristal (TV Series)
(TVE)
Season 1 – Episode 10 (Self)
1984

Matador (Francisco Montesinos)

The Law of Desire (Hardware Store Clerk / Journalist's Voice)

Delirios de amor (TV Series)
(TVE)
Episode *El eterno adolescente*
1989

La mujer de tu vida (TV Series)
(Fernando Trueba PC / TVE)
Episode *La mujer feliz* (Self)
1990

Bad Education (Swimming Pool Cleaner)

Vanity Fair: Killers Kill, Dead Men Die
(Vanity Fair)
6 minutes
Director: Annie Leibovitz
Director of Photography: David Schisgall
Cast: Pedro Almodóvar (The Club Owner), Amy Adams, Ben Affleck, Penélope Cruz, Judi Dench, Robert de Niro, Robert Downey Jr., Kirsten Dunst, Tobey Maguire, Helen Mirren, Julianne Moore, Jack Nicholson, Edward Norton, Sylvester Stallone, Sharon Stone, Naomi Watts, Bruce Willis, Kate Winslet.
2007

Alaska y Mario (TV Series)
(El Terrat / MTV España)
Episodes *Ibiza Mix* and *Huracán Maletas* (Self)
2011-2018

Maricón perdido (TV Series)
(WarnerMedia / El Terrat / Codetma Producciones)
Episode *Recuerda* (Self)
2021

BIBLIOGRAPHY

BOOKS

Acevedo-Muñoz, Ernesto, *Pedro Almodóvar*, London, British Film Institute, 2019.
Allison, Mark, *Un laberinto español: Las películas de Pedro Almodóvar*, Madrid, Ocho y Medio, 2003.
Almodóvar, Pedro, *El último sueño*, Barcelona, Reservoir Books, 2023.
Camarero Gómez, Gloria, *Madrid en el cine de Pedro Almodóvar*, Madrid, Akal, 2019.
Castro, Antonio, *Las películas de Pedro Almodóvar*, Madrid, Ediciones JC, 2010.
D'Lugo, Marvin & Vernon, Kathleen M., *A Companion to Pedro Almodóvar*, Chichester, Blackwell Publishing Ltd., 2013.
Duncan, Paul & Peiró, Bárbara, *The Pedro Almodóvar Archives*, London, Taschen, 2021.
García, Ladis, *Pedro Almodóvar: La película de su vida*, Madrid, Letrame, 2019.
Holguín, Antonio, *Pedro Almodóvar*, Madrid, Cátedra, 2006.
Kercher, Dona, *Latin Hitchcock. How Almodóvar, Amenábar, De la Igesia, Del Toro and Campanella Became Notorius*, London, Wallflower Press, 2015.
Levy, Emanuel, *Gay Directors, Gay Films?*, New York, Columbia University Press, 2015.
Lowenstein, Stephen (Ed.), *Mi primera película*, Barcelona, Alba, 2001.
Markus, Sasa, *La poética de Pedro Almodóvar*, Barcelona, Littera Books, 2001.
Martínez-Carazo, Cristina, *Almodóvar en la prensa de Estados Unidos*, Valencia, Universitat de València, 2017.
Mejean, Jean-Max, *Almodóvar, les femmes et les chansons*, Paris, L'Harmattan, 2011.
Sánchez-Arce, Ana María, *The Cinema of Pedro Almodóvar*, Manchester University Press, 2020.

Sánchez Noriega, José Luis, *Universo Almodóvar: Estética de la pasión en un cineasta posmoderno*, Madrid, Alianza, 2017.
Shulman, Liliana, *Los films de Almodóvar: Un entramado de evocaciones, autobiografía y emociones*, Buenos Aires, Biblos, 2020.
Smith, Paul Julian, *Desire Unlimited: The Cinema of Pedro Almodóvar (Third Edition)*, London, Verso, 2014.
Sotinel, Thomas, *Maestros del cine: Pedro Almodóvar (Spanish Edition)*, Paris, Cahiers du Cinéma, 2010.
Strauss, Frédéric, *Conversaciones con Pedro Almodóvar*, Madrid, Akal, 2001.
Urios-Aparisi, Eduardo, *Puro teatro: Metáfora y espacio en el cine de Pedro Almodóvar*, San Lorenzo de El Escorial, Madrid, Libertarias, 2010.
Vidal, Nuria, *El cine de Pedro Almodóvar*, Madrid, Ministerio de Cultura-ICAA, 1988.

FEATURES AND INTERVIEWS

Almodóvar, Pedro, 'El director cumple diez años', *El Mundo*, 30 October 1989.
Almodóvar, Pedro, 'Génesis de *Kika*', *El País*, 11 May 1993.
Almodóvar, Pedro, 'Epílogo', from the book *Almodóvar: El cine como pasión*, Cuenca, University of Castilla-La Mancha, 2005.
Almodóvar, Pedro, 'El largo viaje hacia la noche', *El Diario.es*, 30 March 2020.
Alonso Franch, Eduardo, 'Medicina, médicos y hospitales en el cine de Almodóvar', Journal of Medicine and Movies, University of Salamanca, January-March 2022.
Alonso G., Agustín, 'Desnudando a Pedro Almodóvar: El Making Of de *Los abrazos rotos*', *Informe Semanal, RTVE*, 12 March 2009.
Álvarez, Juan Francisco, 'La música en el cine de Almodóvar', *Encadenados*, 17 March 2013.
Ander, Álex, 'Pedro me pidió que, con los ojos cerrados, una furtiva lágrima saliera de un ojo para meterse en el otro', *Vanity Fair*, 19 April 2020.
Ander, Álex, 'Historia oral de *Pepi, Luci, Bom...*', *Vanity Fair*, 29 November 2020.
Aparicio, Enrique P., 'Infinitas curiosidades: Julieta Serrano y Benedicta Sánchez', Academia de Cine, 25 March 2020.
Bescós, María, 'Ethan Hawke comparte una imagen con Pedro Pascal anunciando el final del rodaje de *Extraña forma de vida*', *Hobby Consolas*, 3 September 2022.
Bonet Mojica, Lluís, 'Pedro Almodóvar desarrolla en su última película una historia de risas y lágrimas, con Carmen Maura', *La Vanguardia*, 20 July 1984.
Cabrera, Daniel, 'Viaje mitómano a La Mancha de Almodóvar', *El País*, 8 April 2006.
Calvo, Alejandro G., 'Pedro Almodóvar en SensaCine: Del *tacaño* de Ennio Morricone, a su primera vez con Penélope y las escenas míticas que improvisó Carmen Maura', *SensaCine*, 18 October 2021.
Casas, Quim, 'Reencuentro en Bitter Creek', *Dirigido por* 540, June 2023.
Castilla, Amelia, 'Liberto Rabal será el protagonista de la nueva película de Almodóvar', *El País*, 1 February 1997.
Claros, Isabel, '*El matador*, una historia de amor y muerte', *La Vanguardia*, 1 November 1985.
Cobos, Juan, & Marías, Miguel, 'Almodóvar secreto', *Nickel Odeon* 1, Winter 1995.
Crespo, Irene, '*Madres paralelas*: el viaje emocional de Pedro Almodóvar', *Traveler*, 8 October 2021.
Davis, Edward, 'Cate Blanchett says Todd Field's *TAR* is about a fall from grace & talks finally working with Almodóvar', *The Playlist*, 28 April 2022.
De Lucas, Gonzalo, 'El deseo de la actriz. Estética del proceso creativo en los filmes de Almodóvar', from the book *El cine de Almodóvar: Una poética de lo trans*, Sevilla, Universidad Internacional de Andalucía, 2015.
De Pablos, Juan, 'Los cortometrajes de Pedro Almodóvar', *Encadenados*, 12 March 2009.
De Prado, Claudio M., 'Pedro Almodóvar y Tilda Swinton presumen de nueva normalidad en la primera foto del rodaje de *La voz humana*', *GQ*, 16 July 2020.
Del Corral, Pedro, 'Pedro Almodóvar y el pueblo que salvó *Volver*', *La Razón*, 25 July 2019.
Devís, Álvaro, 'El primer largometraje de Almodóvar en inglés, el proyecto frustrado de la nueva Ciudad de la Luz', *Valencia Plaza*, 6 June 2023.
Fernández Rubio, Andrés, '*Átame equivale a Te quiero*, dice Almodóvar de su última película', *El País*, 13 December 1989.
Fernández-Santos, Elsa, 'Pedro Almodóvar rueda *Todo sobre mi madre*, su historia más femenina', *El País*, 24 September 1998.
Fernández-Santos, Elsa, 'La muerte en La Mancha está llena de vida y de gracia', *El País*, 26 June 2005.
Ferrando, Carlos, 'Pedro Almodóvar lleva a cabo su antigua aspiración de hacer un film de hermanos', *Diario 16*, 1 September 1986.
Ferrández Sampietro, Lara, 'La representación de la madre en el cine de Pedro Almodóvar', University of Zaragoza, 2016.
Fiestas, Jorge, & Ferrando, Carlos, '*Entre tinieblas* será la película escándalo del 83', *Diario 16*, 7 March 1983.
Galán, Diego, 'Un País de Cine: *¿Qué he hecho yo para merecer esto!!*', *El País*, 6 February 2004.
García, Rocío, 'Almodóvar reclama la intimidad del dolor', *El País*, 27 October 1993.
García, Yago, 'Los rodajes más conflictivos del cine español', *Cinemanía*, 25 October 2011.
García, Yago, '¿Por qué es *La voz humana* tan importante para Almodóvar?', *Cinemanía*, 12 February 2020.
Gómez Gómez, Agustín, 'Del autorretrato a una cierta autobiografía', from the book *El cine de Almodóvar: Una poética de lo trans*, Sevilla, Universidad Internacional de Andalucía, 2015.
González Miranda, Carolina, 'Dónde se rodó *Julieta*, de Almodóvar', *Traveler*, 8 April 2016.
Guerra, María; Martínez, Luis & Alegre, Luis, 'Encuentro con el público de Pedro Almodóvar en Zaragoza con motivo del Premio Audi Feroz de Honor 2023', 27 January 2023. https://www.youtube.com/watch?v=XSz0oR0LXZ0.
Guzmán, Almudena, 'Penélope Cruz: Soy actriz, no carne de cañón de la prensa rosa', *ABC*, 14 December 1997.
Hernando, Alberto, 'Quién es Milena Smit, la nueva chica Almodóvar', *Esquire*, 27 July 2021.
Herrero, Nacho, 'Días de gloria en Paterna gracias a Pedro Almodóvar', *El Periódico*, 26 January 2020.
Iturribarria, Fernando, '*Hable con ella* es un filme brutalmente lírico y romántico', *Diario 16*, 9 June 2001.
Lázaro, Margarita, '23 datos curiosos que seguro que no conocías de *Dolor y gloria*', *The Huffington Post*, 5 September 2019.
López, Ianko, '*Entre tinieblas*, o cómo Almodóvar finalizó la transición con una historia de monjas, drogas y lesbianismo', *Vanity Fair*, 26 January 2019.
López García, Raquel, '*Los abrazos rotos* es un drama con tintes de cine negro', *Interfilms*, June 2008.
Losa, David, 'Los escenarios de película de Pedro Almodóvar por España', *The Huffington Post*, 16 February 2016.
Madrid, José, '*Volver*, 15 años de la película que reconcilió a Almodóvar y Carmen Maura (y gustó incluso a Boyero)', *Vanitatis / El Confidencial*, 19 March 2021.
Maíllo, J.A., 'Chus Lampreave: Me asusta la vida y hacer cine, por eso solo trabajo con mis amigos', *Diario 16*, 3 February 1986.
Martí, Octavi, 'Almodóvar conquista a Pina Bausch', *El País*, 8 June 2001.
Martínez, Beatriz, '10 curiosidades de *La ley del deseo*, por Pedro Almodóvar', *Fotogramas*, 6 March 2017.
Martínez, Luis, 'Ryuichi Sakamoto: Me arrepiento de lo que hice con Pedro Almodóvar', *El Mundo*, 5 September 2017.
Martínez, Luis, '*Dolor y gloria*: La fiebre del cine perfecto', *El Mundo*, 13 January 2020.
Martínez, Luis, 'Mis vaqueros dicen cosas que nunca se han escuchado en un *western*', *El Mundo*, 27 January 2023.
Medina, Marta, 'Almodóvar en corto: *La voz humana*, una anomalía del cine español', *El Confidencial*, 23 October 2020.
Mengual, Elena, 'Pedro Almodóvar regresa con *Volver*, una comedia en la que mira a la muerte con naturalidad', *El Mundo*, 14 March 2006.
Montano, Alicia G., & Guerra, Manolo, 'Almodóvar: Regreso a la adolescencia', *Informe Semanal, RTVE*, 6 March 2004.
Montano, Alicia G., '*Los amantes pasajeros:* Para mayores sin reparos', *Informe Semanal, RTVE*, 26 February 2013.
Montano, Alicia G., 'Pedro Almodóvar nos habla de *Dolor y gloria*, su película más íntima', *Fotogramas*, 22 March 2019.
Morán López, Ángela, 'Pedro Almodóvar como caso de cine posmoderno a través de seis películas', University of Sevilla, July 2022.
Muñoz, Diego, 'Nuevo Almodóvar, con Carmen Maura transexual y Eusebio Poncela como *alter ego* del director', *La Vanguardia*, 24 August 1986.
Murillo, Noelia, 'Pedro Almodóvar abandona la adaptación de *Manual para mujeres de la limpieza*', *Woman Magazine*, 14 September 2022.
Noriega, David, & Morales, Clara, 'Pedro Almodóvar: Utilizar la pandemia para atacar al gobierno es el peor uso posible de la democracia', *El Diario.es*, 19 October 2020.

Núñez Jaime, Víctor, 'La creación literaria en Almodóvar', *Milenio*, 28 December 2019.
Ortiz, Francisco J., '*Noir* Almodovariano. A propósito de *Carne trémula* y *La piel que habito*', University of Alicante, 2021.
Padalino, Leah, '*La piel que habito*: un thriller *almodovariano*', *La mente es maravillosa*, 7 November 2022.
Pagani, Malcom, 'Pedro Almodóvar: Tutto so di me. I trauma, i vizi, i miei 70 anni, la mia vita', *Vanity Fair Italia*, 15 May 2019.
Parrado, Diego, 'Mujeres al borde de un Stendhalazo', *Revista AD*, 23 March 2018.
Pereira Zazo, Oscar, 'Reseña de *La flor de mi secreto*: Relevancia de la feminidad en la identidad masculina', University of Nebraska-Lincoln, May 2007.
Pinedo, Lucio V., 'Las influencias de Almodóvar', *El Ciudadano*, 2016.
Ponga, Paula, 'No sé cuántas películas me quedan por hacer, noto el paso del tiempo', *Fotogramas*, 4 October 2021.
Porcel, María, 'Emma Suárez y Adriana Ugarte son *Julieta*: sus sorprendentes formas de prepararse para Almodóvar', *The Huffington Post*, 8 April 2016.
Ricci Anduaga, Aníbal, '*Hable con ella:* La ética de un acto de amor', *Cine y Literatura*, 27 May 2020.
Rosado, Ricardo, 'La película de Pedro Almodóvar que inspiró a Quentin Tarantino para cambiar el cine de los 90', *Fotogramas*, 11 August 2022.
Sánchez Alcolea, Marina, 'Risas y lágrimas en *Tacones lejanos*, de Pedro Almodóvar', *RTVE*, 24 July 2021.
Sánchez-Mesa, Domingo, 'Plasticidad de la identidad ciborg en *La piel que habito*', from the book *El cine de Almodóvar: Una poética de lo trans*, Sevilla, Universidad Internacional de Andalucía, 2015.
Sancho Cardiel, Mateo, 'El avión de *Los amantes pasajeros* es una muestra de la España de hoy', *20 Minutos*, 18 February 2013.
Sardá, Juan, 'Las madres de Almodóvar o el amor puro', *El Cultural*, 8 October 2021.
Sartori, Beatriz, 'Esta película me representa por entero', *El Mundo*, 2 February 2002.
Silvestre, Juan, 'Pedro Almodóvar nos da las 8 claves de *Dolor y gloria*', *Fotogramas*, 13 March 2019.
Silvestre, Juan, '12 razones por las que seguimos amando *La mala educación*', *Fotogramas*, 18 March 2019.
Silvestre, Juan, '*Todo sobre mi madre* en 9 curiosidades', *Fotogramas*, 16 April 2019.
Silvestre, Juan, '*La flor de mi secreto:* 10 curiosidades en su 25 aniversario', *Fotogramas*, 22 September 2020.
Silvestre, Juan, 'Fotogramas de Plata 2019: Pedro Almodóvar en *Qué película la de aquel rodaje*', *Fotogramas*, 20 November 2020.
Silvestre, Juan, 'Pedro Almodóvar: Amar en el lejano Oeste', *Fotogramas* 2.156, June 2023.
Sisí Sánchez, Alberto, '*Extraña forma de vida*: Un western en Almería producido por Saint Laurent, el nuevo proyecto de Almodóvar', *Vogue*, 17 August 2022.
Tena, Agustín, 'Pedro Almodóvar dirige en *Laberinto de pasiones* una alta comedia de ficción histórica', *El País*, 25 April 1982.
Tessé, Jean-Philippe, 'Des douleurs, del couleurs, entretien avec Pedro Almodóvar', *Cahiers du Cinéma*, 722, May 2016.
Valdés, Marcela, 'Pedro Almodóvar Is Still Making Movies That Shock', *The New York Times Magazine*, 18 December 2021.
Vallín, Pedro, '*Lo más sensato era abandonar este guion*: El director de cine manchego Pedro Almodóvar estrena este viernes su último trabajo, *La piel que habito*', *La Vanguardia*, 29 August 2011.
Varderi, Alejandro, 'Familias al borde: El cine de Pedro Almodóvar 40 años después', *Viceversa Magazine*, 24 November 2014.
Vega, Cristina, '*Julieta*: La recaudación de lo nuevo de Almodóvar en Francia duplica la taquilla española', *Sensacine*, 14 June 2016.
Vegas, Valeria, 'Las 20 revelaciones de Pedro Almodóvar que hace sobre sí mismo en *Dolor y gloria*', *El Mundo*, 30 March 2019.
Vilar, Màrius, 'El cine de Almodóvar en la taquilla mundial', *Industrias del Cine*, 21 March 2019.
Ximénez, Mario, 'Pedro Almodóvar: Mi vida en 35 milímetros', *Vogue*, 21 March 2019.

ACKNOWLEDGMENTS

The author would like to thank the following people for their invaluable help:

To Rob Nichols and Caterina Favaretto, for entrusting me with such a challenging and exciting project.
To Adelle Mahoney and the Palazzo team, for creating a book beyond all my expectations.
To Antonio Banderas and Cecilia Roth, for sharing their memories and experiences with Pedro.
To Lola García and Sergio Rey, for making the treasures of El Deseo available to me.
To Manuel Outumuro, for sharing with us his fascinating vision of Almodóvar.
To Annabelle Sandwith and María Puchol, for solving all my doubts with the English version.
To Trini Solano and Goyo Ramos, for making possible what seemed impossible.
And, of course, to my wife and children, for the time not shared during all these months. I love you all.

PICTURE CREDITS

T: Top; B: Bottom; L: Left; R: Right
Cover image courtesy of Outumuro Estudio © Manuel Outumuro
Courtesy of Alamy
© El Deseo S.A./AJ Pics 187; © El Deseo S.A./Album 70, 73, 94, 120T; © El Deseo S.A./CIBY 2000/Album 91, 92; © El Deseo S.A./Cinematic 154b; © El Deseo S.A./Entertainment Pictures 116; © El Deseo S.A./Everett Collection Inc 31; © El Deseo S.A./PACO NAVARRO/Album 102; © El Deseo S.A./Photo 12/Archives du 7e Art collection 40; © El Deseo S.A./TCD/Prod.DB 34, 142, 168; © El Deseo S.A./TESAURO/Album 41T; © El Deseo S.A./TESAURO/FIGARO FILMS/Album 24; © El Deseo S.A./TESAURO/KAKTUS/Album 44, 53; © El Deseo S.A. /Collection Christophel 206; © El Deseo S.A./Landmark Media 214, 216, 222T; © Sony Pictures Classics/Entertainment Pictures 208, 219, 222B
Courtesy of El Deseo
Palazzo Editions gratefully acknowledges the assistance and images provided by El Deseo D.A., S.L.U.
© El Deseo D.A., S.L.U. 16, 19, 20, 22; © El Deseo D.A., S.L.U. Ana Muller 36, 38, 41B, 42T, 42B; © El Deseo D.A., S.L.U. Antonio de Benito 14, 46, 48, 50, 52; © El Deseo D.A., S.L.U. Archives du 7e Art 9; © El Deseo D.A., S.L.U. Daniel Martinez 122, 125, 126, 129T, 129BL, 129BR, 131; © El Deseo D.A., S.L.U. Diego Lopez Calvin 150, 153, 154T, 156, 157; © El Deseo D.A., S.L.U. Iglesias Mas 221, 224, 227, 228, 231; © El Deseo D.A., S.L.U. Jean Marie Leroy 104, 107, 108, 111, 112, 115, 119, 120BL, 120BR; © El Deseo D.A., S.L.U. Jorge Aparicio 54, 57, 58, 61, 62, 63, 64, 66, 69; © El Deseo D.A., S.L.U. Jose Haro and Lucia Faraig 180, 182, 184, 188; © El Deseo D.A., S.L.U. Macusa Cores 74, 77, 78, 80T, 80B, 83; © El Deseo D.A., S.L.U. Manolo Pavon 10, 198, 201, 202, 205, 210, 211, 212, 234T; © El Deseo D.A., S.L.U. Miguel Bracho 4, 144, 147T, 147B, 149; © El Deseo D.A., S.L.U. Mimmo Catarinich 84, 86, 88, 96, 99, 101T, 101B; © El Deseo D.A., S.L.U. Nico Bustas 6; © El Deseo D.A., S.L.U. Pablo Perez Minguez 26, 29, 30, 32, 232; © El Deseo D.A., S.L.U. Paola Ardizzoni and Emilio Pereda 2, 13, 158, 160, 162, 165, 166TL, 166TR, 166B, 170, 173, 174, 175, 177, 178, 190, 193, 194, 196, 197, 235; © El Deseo D.A., S.L.U. Teresa Isasi 132, 135, 137, 138, 141, 234B